Gr-sch.

GOT NO TIME TO FOOL AROUND
A Motivation Program for Education

Counseling Center

GOT NO TIME
TO FOOL AROUND

A Motivation Program for Education

by REBECCA SEGAL

THE WESTMINSTER PRESS
Philadelphia

COPYRIGHT © MCMLXXII THE WESTMINSTER PRESS

All rights reserved—no part of this book may be reproduced in any form without permission in writing from the publisher, except by a reviewer who wishes to quote brief passages in connection with a review in magazine or newspaper.

PUBLISHED BY THE WESTMINSTER PRESS®
PHILADELPHIA, PENNSYLVANIA

PRINTED IN THE UNITED STATES OF AMERICA

Library of Congress Cataloging in Publication Data

Segal, Rebecca, 1915-
    Got no time to fool around.

    1. Motivation in education. 2. Education, Urban—United States. I. Title.
LB1065.S44   370.15′4   72-4551
ISBN 0-664-20952-1

This story is dedicated: to hundreds upon
hundreds of students, parents, and teachers who
have given me reason to care about them, and

To Victor, my husband, my alter ego, and
To my grandsons, Billy and Alex, who will
have a better society because of the
quality of the "M" students, and
To Beverly Hendricks, my lovely and talented
young secretary, who delights me with her
humanism

The true test of civilization is, not the census, nor the size of cities, nor the crops, but the kind of man the country turns out.

Ralph Waldo Emerson

Contents

Foreword by Gaylord P. Harnwell	11
Prologue	13
1. The Transformation of Cally Jones	19
2. The Challenge of E. Washington Rhodes	29
3. In the Beginning . . .	44
4. Bridging the Generation Gap	56
5. Building Self-esteem	74
6. Crisis in Discipline	85
7. Rescuing the "Throwaway Child"	100
8. Summer "M" on Campus	117
9. The Environment for Motivation	130
10. Teachers Are Human	136
11. Groton-On-The-Dumps	158
After Thoughts	167
Appendix	175

Foreword

All of America is concerned in the multitude of problems that arise in the enormous, densely packed populations of our major cities. Economic and social forces have powered the high mobility that technology provides, and the free ebb and flow of people of all races, creeds, and cultural levels within our country has led to the extremes of population density that so trouble our own city of Philadelphia. The nature of the difficulties is not novel in history but presents new facets and new urgencies; patience and time seem to shorten when people are crowded ever more closely together.

In 1959, The West Philadelphia Corporation was formed by certain eleemosynary institutions that were concerned for the health, welfare, and economic and cultural growth of West Philadelphia. The promotion of readily available public education of high quality was among the Corporation's first priorities. Ten years ago, the Corporation's executive director, Leo Molinaro, and Mrs. Rebecca Segal, then at the West Philadelphia High School, found a very broad and constructive area of mutual concern for a new direction in the educational system, which was faltering sadly under the pressure of the times and circumstances.

Education properly conceived is a lifelong process of which

the public grade schools are only the formal beginning. Philosophically, the most important contribution of our schools should be to awaken the desire to learn and to inculcate a habit of learning. This is a dynamic process which grows with individual involvement as understanding deepens. Striking the spark that initiates this process and nurturing it to a flame that will enlighten subsequent years depends upon the motivation that can be aroused in each individual.

The insight that Mrs. Segal has brought to the art of motivating boys and girls in their early years and the enthusiasm and diligence with which she has developed a program that has spread widely through the Philadelphia public school system, until it now reaches many thousands of students, are attested by the contents of this book.

Benjamin Disraeli's admonition to the House of Commons nearly a hundred years ago, "Upon the education of the people of this country the fate of this country depends," is as applicable to our country and today. We are all greatly indebted to Mrs. Segal and her associates for the important contribution to the educational process in Philadelphia that is set forth in this volume.

GAYLORD P. HARNWELL
Chairman
　The West Philadelphia Corporation
President Emeritus
　The University of Pennsylvania

Prologue

Man is by nature a sanguine creature. I suppose that if he were not, the human race would have phased itself out a long time ago. Our hopefulness, our need to produce and progress, make life bearable and enjoyable for ourselves and, in the end, bearable for those around us.

Those of us engaged in education, social welfare, law, and a hundred allied fields were all saying the same words as we turned into the '60s from a half century of incredible scientific advancement with but relatively little human progress. We agreed that as a nation we were heading for trouble: that all we were doing was building a country without building a nation; that people were the stuff of which a nation is made; that the very essence of our nationhood, the Bill of Rights, was being subverted by our lack of perception and concern and that we'd waited too long to undo the wrongs of the past.

Then in the '60s we all perceived as if by a signal that one of our most grievous faults was that we had no communication—we had no dialogue with each other. We had lived in mental ghettos too long. To compensate we broke out nationally in a rash of dialogue of all kinds: sensitivity sessions, lecture and discussion, all with the avowed purpose of communicating in an effort to cure our ills. We talked for hundreds of thousands of hours; we "communicated."

But nobody was listening. Nobody paid attention. No one was hearing with understanding and care. It took four assassinations, three major presidential commissions—ignored and shelved—riots and demonstrations, to bring us to the realization that our trouble is our unfeeling and hate for each other, which has germinated the violence, and perhaps the eventual destruction of our nation. As a people we degraded men persistently until we destroyed their belief in themselves, their humanity and their essentiality to the life of others. We had made them "untouchables" even to themselves, as Hitler had done to those Jews who went to the gas chambers. Yet so regenerative is the human spirit that, given a hope of hope, a man will come to life, just as the same remnants of Europe's Jews were able to regenerate and produce the state of Israel. Given the knowledge that he is in a mutuality with his fellowman, he will enrich his surroundings.

For three years in the late '50s I served as the national president of Women's American ORT (Organization for Rehabilitation through Training), traveling abroad widely to know the needs of the schools and the students. My experiences with the communities supporting them provided me with affirmation of my own philosophy. I came to believe that all human beings, no matter what their origin, their religion, their politics, are intrinsically alike: they react to love, hunger, pain. They respond with almost predictable reactions to various stimuli in the achievement of certain goals. The Jew and the Arab in the ORT school in Marrakech bloomed under an affectionate hand and a word of praise. The Moslem and the Jewish Persian ORT students found they could do a difficult exercise with the lathe when they were convinced that they were capable.

Avi, a boy in the Jerusalem ORT school in 1953, had survived the Nazi camps and wandered hungry over the face of Europe. Desolate, his personality twisted, he presented a wall, so that the teachers in ORT-Jerusalem could find no way to him. He distrusted and disbelieved everyone. Nothing interested him, until one day his electricity teacher praised his progress and gave him a special problem in wiring. It was then the young man's life began to change—because of a simple thing: a word of kindness and praise.

I was visiting ORT-Jerusalem that year, 1953. The country was five years old, besieged by seven Arab nations, 120 million Arabs against 1 million Israelis. Everything was rationed—food, clothing, electricity. At eight o'clock each evening all unnecessary power was turned off. After eight one evening I was meeting with the school's director when we became aware of someone scolding loudly. I accompanied the director down the stairway to the basement. There, tucked away in a dark alcove, was Avi, bent under a simple, naked lamp bulb, being berated by his teacher. The facts came out. He knew he had done wrong, that he was not allowed to be back in school using the electricity. But for the first time in his life he had become enchanted with what he was doing and couldn't wait to complete his experiment. This was his moment of readiness and motivation.

My observations regarding human response and motivation were founded on the idea that people are alike; on incidents that had taken place in other lands with people of widely different backgrounds, religions, cultures, and economic strata.

The majority of Jews and Moslems of Morocco, of Iran, live in quarters or ghettos that are meaner, more degrading to the human spirit, than any of America's urban pestholes. Set usually in the center of the ancient cities, these mellahs and the counterpart Arab medinas (for the life of the poor Arab is little different from that of the poor Jew) are the rotted core from which radiates, within earshot, a city with pastel, rich villas. These are the inheritance from the colonial powers, the great maggots which fed on the bodies of poverty.

When I first became acquainted with the people in the mellahs of North Africa, I wondered what it would take, if it were at all possible, to erase the fear of life and their despair. What could be done to give them a sense of tomorrow, a hope perhaps, that one did not have to live out one's life in the same abject misery as one's forebears had endured for hundreds of years? What familial support could they give their children? What hope?

If I thought I had seen the most degrading human existence in those mellahs from Persia to Morocco, I was to be stunned by yet another sight from which I thought there could be no redemption. I traveled south from Marrakech into the Atlas Mountains where people lived like troglodytes in carved-out burrows of the mountainside; at Imi-n-Tanout I saw Jews who had lived this way for two thousand years since the dispersion from Palestine, having become even more primitive than the state from which they had come. The whole panorama had a mythological quality, yet here in reality was a cave dweller who wore a yarmulke, the traditional skullcap. I was brought through a door, no more than a slab across the opening, painted blue in Arab tradition to ward off the evil eye, and led by candle down a long stone passage. We entered what was certainly a dwelling. There were cushions on the stone floor and a mattress in a corner. The stench was unbearable; a French drain in the far corner was their toilet. And into this miserable scene a new baby had just exited from the mother. Voracious flies, such as one sees only in the Middle East and Far East, were already attached to the infant, in its eyes; trachoma would be the result. More flies on every inch of skin. No effort was made to brush the flies away. It had to be thus. One had to adjust in Morocco—adjust to four out of every ten babies dying in the first year; at best, living to the old age of thirty-five with trachoma, blindness, ringworm, and without hope.

Yet, the father (I had thought him to be an old man, a grandfather, perhaps) asked what we could do to get him to Marrakech. Even Marrakech, sixty miles north, a city—even that degrading mellah would be an improvement, a step up. Where had he gotten his aspiration? How had his goal been born?

A huge apartment complex built outside Casablanca fronting the Atlantic Ocean was pointed out to me. It had been constructed as new housing for the ghetto dwellers—except, how could they pay such high rents? Even if they could have a refrigerator and a real stove instead of a kerosene plate, the whole thing was a dream.

The dream became a reality for a few families whose sons had been trained in the ORT school. The money they earned in a month was more than fathers had earned in six months, a year. A skill could do this miraculous thing. Now there was motivation. One could aspire to new goals. Parents could urge on their young to try harder, to overcome adolescent apathy which is normal even when one is not of a depressed and hopeless minority. A new dimension had been added to the parents' horizons. The mute acceptance of a God-given, fateful poverty need not be. One could be a good Jew, a religious one, and still improve one's lot in life. Dignified, yet frightened fathers in their long Moroccan djellabas and wooden clogs, with the omnipresent skullcap, stood in line with their sons to register in the vocational school. Often there was disappointment because all available places were gone for the year. And this "hard to get" aspect of the commodity made its achievement even more prestigious and desirable. How significant was the kiss placed on the father's hand by an appreciative son as they bid farewell in the court of the school. With what hopefulness a father could return to grinding poverty.

Our nation has been a symbol of hope for millions in the past. That's what it's all about. Hope. And that's what this story is about. It is a story of education and what it can and should mean to man in enriching his days on earth; it tells about the struggle to change hard and hateful opinions about fellow Americans different from ourselves. It's a story about the goals and aspirations of people—adolescents, parents, and schoolmen —in the context of their social and human problems. It's the negation of elitist educators who say that "education should be for those, only, who want it; that mass education has outlived its usefulness"—this heresy in a country that depends for its very system of government on the educated judgment of its citizens.

It is the antithesis of new young "educationists" who perceive of existing educational programs as totally bad and every educator over thirty as "out to lunch."

This program, the Motivation Program, is a demonstration that, in the true sense of the word "educate," we can "lead out to learning" by supplying hope and by learning the techniques by which a human being reaches his "moment of motivation." It lives by the dictum that it is never too late to learn; that we must feel needed and wanted and that "the caring is all."

> Being designated as a member of a select program has a positive effect on the student's image and his desire to achieve the goals.

1

The Transformation of Cally Jones

Cally Jones is a statistic, in many ways. In fact, his number was one of 284,000 Philadelphia school children each with his own problems but some of them having more hopeless, bleak existences and futures than did others.

At fourteen, Cally had many of the same distresses that most of his friends had. Black, on the edge of violent militancy, the oldest child in a welfare family of his mother and five other children, he had never known any kind of joy. Oh yes, he remembered when he was much younger the pleasure he'd felt when his father had appeared on infrequent returns to the family. But even as he remembered, Cally felt the fist of fear in his stomach, the mental image of his drunken father staggering around the house for a few days drinking up the pennies left over from the check. He never brought any money home with him; only took.

Everybody in the house suffered during his father's homecomings: the kids who caught the beatings for just being alive; Cally's mother for getting knocked up year after year in rhythm with his father's visits; finally, Cally, who hid during the visits, hid in the house or in abandoned houses of the neighborhood so he'd not get beaten up, so he'd not suffer the father's jealousy, the jealousy toward his only son.

Cally at fourteen was a tall, skinny, gangling kid, his legs all knobs, his middle a snakehips girdle, and his bony chest the nearest thing to a xylophone. He was undernourished, underfed, and always hungry. His dark, brown eyes regarded the world around him softly, looking for friendship and love from everybody, anybody. He needed this one ingredient more than everything, but it was the thing he would never get from his mom or his father, for sure.

He had a dim memory of being hugged by his grandmother down home in South Carolina. It was a good feeling that came back to him, but it was good and dim—nine years ago. Then they'd all packed up and come to Philadelphia 'cause the pickin's were better. But they weren't. His father took off, leaving him, his sisters, and his pregnant mother. That's how it went, year after year. For some reason his mother didn't like him, and it saddened Cally to know this. It wasn't hard to gather this. Little things—torn shirt or pants or underwear that was urine-yellow beyond washing, bought in a rummage sale. A sweater that was always stiff as a board, the wool ruined by washing and shrinking. He felt like a derelict all the time in school. Or else his mother brought home cast-off clothes from the houses she cleaned. The first time he got his own jacket, new for him, was when his teacher in junior high school gave him a job around his house. With that first money he bought his first coat. What a feeling it was! His mother beat the stuffin's out of him when he brought it home. But he had it. He'd worn it home and she couldn't make him return it.

It was the first taste of green that made him want to drop out of school and go to work. He hated everything except his history class. Mr. Feldman made world cultures the only bright spot of the day, with the Trojan horse and Charlemagne and Hannibal, who was a black man. No other teacher knew that. Cally asked them all. That was it. Mr. Feldman somehow knew what it felt like being black and poor, but he never gave the boy the feeling that the clothes meant anything or that Cally's blackness was a condition different from his own. Why did he know about Cally? The teacher didn't have everything going for him either.

The Transformation of Cally Jones

Most of the kids called him Charley Jew and made the history class a shambles. Feldman at fifty—fat, tired, bald—had twenty-five years of teaching in the city, and only now was he beginning to feel that the time for his exit from the classroom had come. He had one class of children in the day who were respectful and who wanted to learn. They were the stars. All black, they were offspring of residents who had not yet deserted their beautiful upper West Philadelphia and Wynnefield neighborhoods. His remaining four classes were a potpourri of severely undereducated, socially maladjusted, and, in some cases, incapable children. Even so, Joe Feldman felt he could get them to want to learn. Year after year he persevered. He was about to give up. It was kids like Cally who kept him going. If only he could get the boy to hold on and not drop out. Cally knew he'd miss Feldman's class, 'cause it was the only place where he was the star. He didn't even have to study; only read. He devoured the books about the past that Mr. Feldman lent him. And he was a good reader. But everything else stank. He hated going to school. It was a waste of time.

Mr. Feldman pleaded with him.

"Cally, you're a very smart guy. You proved it to yourself this whole year, didn't you?" Cally remained silent.

"I know you don't enjoy a lot of your classes, but you gotta stay and try to drink it up. Are you listening?"

"Yeah, I'm listenin'. But I hate ta come in ta mosta the teachers' rooms. I feel lousy an'en I fall asleep. An'en they send me down to the vice-principal."

"Well, what do you think they oughta do, give you stars for falling asleep in every class?"

"It ain't my fault. I'm always tired. I get up tired and stay that way all day."

"I told you plentya times you don't eat right. All that cake and Coke for breakfast I see you eating will ruin your stomach! And running around with the fellas till twelve o'clock at night. How do you expect to keep your motor in good condition with the way you mistreat it? How can you keep your brain fit?"

"Aah!" Cally's laughter squealed raucously, deprecatingly.

And that's all Joe Feldman could do with Cally about his eating and sleeping habits. But he did get the kid's promise to go on to Overbrook High School and to get into the Motivation Program so he could prepare for college, a crazy idea of Feldman's. He was always searching for kids like these.

It was Joe Feldman's urging and talking, his obvious affection for the kid, his respect for the youngster's mind, that gave Cally the strength to take the first difficult step. He buckled down that last report period just enough to squeak through and be promoted. He had to run the gauntlet as he walked home with the little hop and jump that was the gait of the gang; or when he went roaming with them, the "gangster" would be sucking his thumb to lessen his fear. The gang saw something different about him now. He wasn't willing to spend limitless hours with them. He'd promised Mr. Feldman. He had to prove he could do it for Feldman.

The important thing to Cally about his getting into the Motivation Program at Overbrook High was that it felt as though Mr. Feldman had personally handed him over to Mrs. Bortnicker and that she had become an extension of Mr. Feldman.

That first half of the tenth year was almost more than Cally could overcome. His father had come home a few times, squeezing as much as he could out of his mother's purse. He came home drunk, beat the whole house, his worn-out wife, Cally, who stayed out of the house as much as he could, and the girls, who were all ages and underfoot in the two-room apartment. Cally's mother even caught her husband pulling Evie, the thirteen-year-old daughter, into bed. Then she threw him out, threatening to get the police. After he left for his sojourn, the family could return to normal, Cally sleeping on the pile of dirty clothes in the chipped, claw-footed bathtub, three of the girls on a mattress in the area that served as kitchen, living room, and dining room, and two others in bed with their mother.

The kitchen table, always redolent of the last meal with scraps of leftover food and curious animal life examining it,

The Transformation of Cally Jones 23

was Cally's desk as he studied for the next day. He found it impossible to concentrate, however, with the family milling around, fighting, yelling, arguing. He took to hiding his books between his mother's spring and mattress while he was at school to preserve them from the young children's hands.

Mrs. Bortnicker, to whom Mr. Feldman had sent him, asked him deep questions. The Motivation Office was a long, narrow cloakroom on the fourth floor of Overbrook High, converted for the special program. Into this space were jammed, railroad style, three teacher's desks. The first was the secretary's, the second the cultural organizer's, and the back one, separated from the others by a partition, was the coordinator's private office. It was private only insofar that no one could see who was at Mrs. Bortnicker's desk. What was being said was available to all ears unless one was whispering. This, to a large extent, was how Mrs. Bortnicker was talking with Cally.

"You've been in Overbrook two months, Cally. How are you finding things? Your report shows that you've passed all subjects, but just barely. You're absent a bit too much. How do you feel about everything?" Cally looked at Mrs. Bortnicker shyly, his tall, angular form and stringy legs seeking a comfortable position in the tiny "office." It was to become his haven in the next three years. The woman before him was white, Jewish, about forty-five years old, with a real body. That was the first thing most people noticed about her, and that the miniskirts showed her off to advantage. Her face might have been beautiful in her youth, but Cally could see that she must have plenty of problems of her own. Maybe that's why a guy got the feeling he could talk to her, like to Mr. Feldman. And that little office with the closed door was open to every one of the 450 kids in the Motivation Program. If Mrs. Bortnicker was busy and the problem couldn't wait, a guy could talk to Mrs. Greenbaum or Mrs. Jarosh.

So here was Cally, who'd been called out of class for the first "check-in meeting." Cally's timid brown eyes met Mrs. Bortnicker's innocent-looking blue ones. Her mop of unruly blond hair, puffed out stylishly, looked like a halo. He liked calling her Mrs. B., as all the seniors did.

"Cally?"

"About the absences—I stayed out to baby-sit when my mother went to the welfare office a few times and on the other days when she went to the clinic." It was easy to talk to her.

"Is your mother sick?"

"Naah, she's gawna have another baby."

"Are you fighting with the fellas on the street? Why is your face so marked up with bruises?"

"It's not the fellas. I don't fight on the street. I ain't been doin' that since I promised Mr. Feldman last year."

"So what happened to you?" She didn't push at a fella. Her blue eyes just looked sad and her pretty face had a smile. You could talk to her. It was almost like to Mr. Feldman. You knew Mrs. Bortnicker wouldn't rat on you or think you were an ignorant nigger for what you told her.

"It was my father. He was home again. And I couldn't keep outa his way."

So that was it. Flip Bortnicker felt a revulsion for a beast of a man who could give this pain to his son, who could damage this child's self.

"I tried to do my lessons and it made him sore so he beat me up. But it's the last time, Mrs. Bortnicker." Cally's face became a dark red as he relived his anger. "It's the last time! I held his hands after he'd given it to me, and I told him he'd never do it again; that I'd beat him to a pulp if I ever saw him touch any of the family again. But I saw how he hates me, Mrs. Bortnicker." Cally shut up as if he'd caught himself, by his recital, in an unforgivable act of betrayal. He'd taken the family's problems out of the house. Mrs. Bortnicker looked away and shuffled some papers on her desk to give Cally time to compose himself.

"Listen, friend, there's a whole business I can't help you with; only you can. There's another area your counselor will do for you. But some things we can do right away. You've begun showing that Mr. Feldman was right. You're a smart kid, and if you'll work with us, if you'll care about yourself, you'll make it." Cally looked deep into the blue eyes to test them for honesty. Then he dropped his own. "If he'd care about himself!" He said this to Mrs. Bortnicker not as a statement—more as a question.

"It's true, Cally. We don't always care enough about ourselves; we aren't always our own best friends. That's the first thing I must convince you about—that you're someone special, so good we want you to go to college. We think you can become a leader in some field."

It was an astounding speech hitting his ear. He'd heard her say things like this to all the kids at the Motivation meeting. But he'd made a secret note to himself that she meant some of the others; now she was saying it to him, specifically. He had an incredible sensation—embarrassment, as if he'd been caught in some alien situation. Yet at the same time he felt a sudden maturity, almost like his chest puffing out with a deep, healthy breath.

"You and I are going to make a pact. We'll always be honest with each other. Whatever we feel, we'll tell. O.K.?" Cally felt his head nodding in agreement. He wanted the pact.

"First, we'll arrange your roster so you can get all your classes compressed into the morning. Then, I want you to bring along your lunch, get a box of milk and come up here. Any corner that's free at any time will be yours. If I'm out, you're to come in here to study. I want all B's on your June report. You're having trouble with geometry? I'll arrange for tutoring. Next, on your way out, stop and talk to Mrs. Greenbaum about your participation in the cultural activities. Get a calendar of events."

"Aah, Mrs. B., I don't dig that stuff. I like rock."

"That's O.K., Cally. We don't all dig the same thing, but if you're going to enrich your own life, you have to experience all kinds of art. And you can go to rock concerts too. We want you to take advantage of the trips in the city and out of town;

classes at the colleges. We want you to spend an evening with adults who are interested in you as a human being, not as a potential doctor or judge or tailor—just a man." Mrs. Bortnicker slowed down, afraid she was coming on too strong.

"Would your mother come to the monthly 'M' Parents meeting?"

"Naah, she ain't interested."

" 'Isn't,' Cally, not 'ain't.' O.K. We'll get started. You have specially rostered classes in English and math beyond your normal roster. Soak it up. When you begin getting your A's and B's, your counselor will give you money, scholarship help. Are we in business?" Mrs. Bortnicker had extended her hand and Cally had grasped it in his huge black paw. He had never before felt the intimate touch of a white person and it was a stunning feeling in his stomach. He walked out of the cubicle with a resolution having formed in his consciousness. He remembered a phrase from the brochure he'd gotten from Mr. Feldman in junior high, describing the Motivation Program. The Program wanted to provide the students with "the moment of motivation." Mr. Feldman in junior high had been the first one to wake him up. But Mrs. Bortnicker made him feel like a man—great. If only his resolution would hold.

By June, Cally had all B's in all subjects. It didn't happen just that easily. Teachers had to be met with, those who had "M" students. If they were to be effective teachers, they had to know much more than their geometry or biology or French. They had to understand the boys and girls in the "M" class. They had to know, really know, what the students' problems were: why did the Callys come in late, tired? What about Cally's records? Did the fact that Cally was a flunker, a repeater and a disturber in his earlier years determine and bias his Overbrook High teachers? Could their bias be turned around, productively?

Cally was an honor roll student all through his junior and senior years. He was an active participant in the varied cultural activities the "M" Program arranged. By the senior year, he'd taken a tenth year "M" student on as a pal, trying to transfer his "moment of motivation."

One week into the new year, Cally's father came home drunk and abusive. Seeking to avoid a fight and to finish his term paper Cally spent the whole evening at the University of Pennsylvania library. When he got home, he found his mother and sisters bruised and angry, having lived through another physical bout. His father had gone out to drink. Cally was livid with rage and wanted to go after him. But his mother, with a foulness of mouth Cally had now become unaccustomed to, told him to stay out of her affairs. She didn't need him to butt in. Cally waited in a fury and finally fell asleep as he lay in the bathtub surrounded by the rancid smell of soiled clothes.

Perhaps it was the very absence of the vibration caused by the breathing of seven people. Cally awakened to the intense quiet. The rooms were empty of people and every stitch of clothing.

A note written by Evie for their mother told a simple tale:

Dear Cally:
  We're goin' down home to grama's with Papa and Mama. Take care of yourself. See you soon.

                                    The Family

Another note from Evie, herself, told him warmly:

  I love ya, Cally. Take care of yourself.

                              Your sister for ever.
                              Evie

Cally was stunned for an hour, shocked to the point where he was late coming to school. He arrived in a dazed state of mind.

Within a few hours a temporary solution to his problem was set up. A teacher, anonymous, who related well to the students and had a little money, set up a small bank account for Cally to draw on. Another teacher invited the young man to stay with him.

Cally got the support he needed in this crucial moment. He was graduated with honor roll status, and received a complete four-year scholarship to college. For two years, Cally has been on the dean's list, a well-adjusted, productive young man.

A week ago Mrs. B. received the annual report from the officials of the various colleges concerning the progress of the "M" students. Among other things, the vice-president wrote:

"Cally is a fine man, intelligent and attractive. More than that, he's an excellent human being. It will please you to know that he's been voted one of the six men in the entire state to be sent to England for his junior year, in political science." Mrs. Bortnicker sent this letter to me, proudly.

As usual when I am dealing with my "M" students, I become totally involved and "subjective," as the cynics call it. As it happens, I have leaped ahead in time to the present. This was an epochal event in Cally's life, planted, nurtured, and brought to bloom by the Motivation Program, an idea within a school. It was an idea and a hope projected by people working in the Program who had invested their lives in others back in late 1962 in its place of origin, West Philadelphia High School, one of many urban high schools in American cities whose sudden change in population had also changed the character of the school.

With proper promotion, even "eggheadism" can become a desirable motive for the peer group.

2

The Challenge of E. Washington Rhodes

Eugene Washington Rhodes, Esq., publisher of *The Philadelphia Tribune,* the foremost black newspaper, stood on the platform of the West Philadelphia High School assembly dispensing awards to the class of 1961. Handsome, powerful, he was the first black appointee to the Board of Education. His appearance this morning therefore was a coup for the principal; this gentlemen would bestow the honors on a high school that had turned 92 percent black within the short space of two to three years.

Nine hundred eleventh- and twelfth-graders sat before him in an auditorium built and furnished in 1912, dark-paneled, dirty; black, broken seats nailed to filthy hardwood floors. It was insisted that nothing needed changing or improving, in these forty-nine years; that the depression budget for the renovation of schools was still functional; that what was good then was still plenty good. So the walls were dark gray with decades of city grime, the benches stripped of the veneer by the sheer stress of traffic. Naked bulb lamps hooded by a fine crystal shade from the high vaulted ceiling produced a sleep-inducing torpor in the students.

Mr. Rhodes looked out over the vast assembly of black faces before him. Every now and then a pink skin leaped out, made doubly prominent by the constant blackness of row upon row of dark-skinned girls and boys. He turned around to look at the thirty-five students who sat behind him; all had returned to their seats after filing before him to accept the award designated for a spectacular feat. Eight white girls and boys had been granted prizes for excellence in scholarship. Twenty-six boys and girls, handsome, Negro, had been handed letters and pins for athletic prowess—football, basketball, gymnastics. One lone Negro boy had taken a scholarship prize. The presentations were over. Mr. Rhodes turned back to the audience, which had cheered lustily as the twenty-six had come forward to take their prizes, but feebly as the nine had stood for their commendation. Sadly he stared out at the mass of upturned faces, stared and shook his head. Quietly, without the fire which his naturally booming voice possessed, he spoke into the mike.

"I came today pleased that I had been asked to officiate at such an event. It always gives me pleasure to see the development of young people and to participate with youth. But I want you to know that this is one of the saddest days I've had in many years." The faces of the principal and other administrators turned sharply toward the speaker, astonished to hear such a dour introduction to his talk. A small incipient hum in the audience, too, was hushed suddenly to listen to this unorthodox introduction.

"Thirty-five students came up to me for awards. Of these, only one for brains was a Negro. One! Look around you! Everybody, look, I say! Turn your heads!" Obeying Mr. Rhodes's command, every head turned to the left and to the right. "How many white faces do you see in the audience? Not many, huh? You know why? Because they're all up here taking prizes for academic excellence, for having brains, that's why! How many Negroes got prizes for that, tell me! One!" His voice had risen and roared so that the mike was overloaded with the sound and the boom of the speaker's anger.

"Are you normal people?" He went on, gaining momentum as he gained anger.

The Challenge of E. Washington Rhodes

"Almost three thousand students in a school and all you could squeeze out was one student who could compete with whites? I'm ashamed. I'm humiliated to have to call myself a Negro in the presence of such a humiliating display of ignorance and mediocrity!" He left the mike and stepped forward to the edge of the platform. His fist clenched, he leaned over the bank of lights, glaring at the faces below him. Even without the mike his voice sailed up to the balcony in back.

"You're good enough to be athletes 'cause all that takes is muscle. But you evidently have no muscle in your brain. You have nothing. You're a disgrace to me and to the Negro people. Now I'm promising you something." Mr. Rhodes shook his fist at an awed assembly. "This is the last time you'll see me here until you can show me you're normal human beings, and can match white people. Don't ever invite me back until you can do that. I'm disgusted with you!" His face gray-black with fury, Eugene Washington Rhodes stalked off the stage with a distressed principal in tow. There was no applause. What would it have been for? An aura of awe, and of incomprehension too, sat like a pall over the assembly. Soon the commanding bell summoned the nine hundred to the beginning of the day's classes and to the normal humdrum. And the unpleasantness in the auditorium could be forgotten. It wasn't, however.

Actually, Mr. Rhodes started a small revolution in the school, and as the years went on, throughout the system. Although at the time he could not have foreseen what his anger and the gauntlet he'd thrown down was to start, he it was, nevertheless, who provoked the principal and a few of his excellent staff to examine what was happening to the students of his school, provoked and challenged and inspired them to do something for a problem about which they had only intellectualized.

Four years later, in the spring of 1965, in a school that had become 98 percent black, Eugene Washington Rhodes returned to make good his promise. All outward appearances were the same. Although the Gothic auditorium had received a well-deserved paint job, the depressive climate still existed. The important difference in the scene lay in the composition of the group seated on the stage. Mr. Rhodes was introduced by the same principal, Jack Neulight, and the guest stepped forward to the mike. He told the audience he was changing the format and would make his brief remarks before the awards were distributed.

It was he who told the story of his humiliation on the same stage in 1961. He repeated the tale of his anger and that he had washed his hands of West Philadelphia High School students. He told them of his promise never to return until they had proved that they had the "same abilities and were normal like whites." Then, with a jubilant, resonant voice, Mr. Rhodes began the presentation of awards of orange W's for excellence in scholarship to twenty-four Negro and three white students of honor roll status, and eleven black students who had merited the presentation of the Distinguished Scholarship Award.

It might have been the way he'd built up the story in his introductory talk; it might have been his evident pleasure—perhaps it was these facts together with the students' pride in their remarkable Negro speaker. What transpired was a momentous event.

As Eugene Washington Rhodes finished the awards, he asked all on the stage to stand together. And as they rose, the entire body of students in the audience, nine hundred, juniors and seniors, a cross section of the school, jumped to their feet and stood clapping their hands wildly to convey to their schoolmates on the stage their appreciation of the honors they had won. For two minutes they stood and applauded this new concept: that Negroes could pursue and achieve scholastic excellence as well as athletic excellence. By their applause they were signifying that they were the normal people Mr. Rhodes had told them about and that the rewards the whites received were possible and obtainable for all who wanted and sought to achieve them. Those on the stage had gotten the message and had taken the reward. Many students left that assembly with a new feeling of self, of caring about one another. For many this warm experience was the motivation toward productivity of one kind or another.

For those on the stage, for Mr. Neulight and his staff, for me especially, this awards assembly was the first crop in the rich harvest produced by careful husbandry in the new program we called the Motivation Program of West Philadelphia High School.

What was needed to bring about the change that Mr. Rhodes demanded in 1961 was readiness, and the time had not yet come to West Philadelphia High School, nor indeed to our society. But enough questions were being asked even before Mr. Rhodes by some parents, alumni, teachers, administrative and community leaders in West Philadelphia to prepare the ground for what had to become a movement. There had to be the readiness for a change in concept, philosophy, and aspiration. The philosophy for change would need leadership and drive. The administration had to be ready. Jack Neulight, our principal, who had brought the problem to a head, and Dr. Alec Washco and Dr. Joseph Brancato, two fine men and vice-principals, were ready. That's what the year 1961-62 was to be for us at West Philadelphia High.

And for me as well. I was teaching English to eleventh- and twelfth-year students and to modified classes, which was a euphemism for the utterly declassed. This was my first year at West, an assignment I had asked for to the amazement of the examiners and administration when I decided to enter full time into the school system. Although I had taken short-term and long-term subbing runs in the junior and senior high schools over a twenty-year period, I had been unwilling to detach myself entirely from one of my keen interests, ORT (Organization for Rehabilitation through Training), a vocational school system for depressed young Jews throughout the world. During these many years, therefore, my life was a happy one filled with the raising of a family, the teaching of music, French, and English to adolescents (an age group I love), and working for adolescents of ORT in far-flung countries. (And in-between, I was singing professionally when I had time.)

That first year at West Philadelphia High I learned about human beings of our own cultures, but it was a year of coming very close to the sad, often helpless lives of one hundred and eighty Negro and four white high school children who came to my class every day for English. Each day was a full and exhausting one in which every emotion was experienced. It was especially so with the homeroom.

I have a theory which I've tested out for many years concerning the coincidence of personalities who congregate in a given class, mass, or audience.

My homeroom that first half year had a coincidence of impossible kids. In all my years in the classroom, in the most difficult junior high schools (which I had always considered a major educational blunder), I had never had any difficulty controlling a class. An experienced teacher has a memory bank of tricks. And I always ran a tight ship without being repressive. This year I met my worst adversary. I hated coming to school. Each morning was a drag. If only I could come in at 9:45 A.M. and bypass this monster of a homeroom group, the entire group.

Nobody ever had any work to prepare for any classes—all had done it the night before! I came to learn, as I recorded the students' subject grades on report cards, that not only had they done no work the night before, but not at all, ever. Since most of the mothers had left for work before the students left for school, there was no breakfast. Instead, they bought steak sandwiches with live onions, Cokes, and Danish, and these unrelated, unsynchronized smells hovered over our heads, saturating our hair and clothing with the heady onion.

All period I was bombarded by a symphony of gum clackers, smackers, bubble blowers. It was maddening, and the more I complained, the greater satisfaction the students took in the activity. There was constant socializing, moving around, horsing around, calling, laughing, braying. Each day was renewed trauma. It was an unfortunate coincidence of thirty-eight wild kids in the alphabetical family of Joneses and Johnsons. And, probably, the reason for the disorder was to be found in the teacher's being tied up with roll-taking, absentee-note recording, collecting for Kim Sung, a Korean orphan, or for the Red Cross, or for a half dozen other drives. The period was a wrecker, and it would take me a half hour to unscramble my nerves after the students had left. Nor was I entirely rid of them until the next day—like the bad penny, a Jones or a Johnson would come to haunt me during the day. Leon Jones had "got caught short" behind the stage. He'd defecated and used the elegant, moth-eaten, velvet curtain for his cleaner. Sara Johnson was caught on the rarely traveled third-to-fourth-floor stairway getting her lesson in sex education. Practical demonstration, after all—a picture is worth a thousand words. Somehow the other teachers and the administration were holding me responsible for the bad manners.

From 9:45 to 9:49 I had four minutes of minding the halls outside my door to see that the students kept the traffic moving quickly. Well, more quickly. The school occupied a huge site four blocks square and had four floors. Frequently students had the total acreage to cover in the four minutes. What with stopping or slowing for a chat here or a laugh there, lateness to class was a serious problem. One illiterate English teacher "couldn't stop the kids conjugating around her." I didn't mind monitoring. It was part of the job, on the same level with the shades being drawn at the same height, every piece of paper on the floor taken immediately to the wastebasket. It was all part of being a real good professional. These were philosophies of principals of that vintage. "A good teacher is never without a piece of chalk in every pocket."

From 9:42 to 2:30 I had one class after another which produced varied degrees of satisfaction. An attempt had been made at homogeneous grouping, so, more or less, the classes were rapid, mediocre, or modified. Only, it wasn't always possible. Errors occurred often, and they were hurtful to the kids in a wrong group and to the teacher who didn't know to whom she should cater.

The vulnerable pupil or teacher was thrown into a class of thirty-eight average students, all Negro, children who may not have come to school to learn but were for the most part docile, respectful, and obedient, reverting to the normal state only when they were let loose on a weak substitute. Within any given class there were a few exhibitionists who had to respond vocally to any and every incident in the class with some ribaldry which frequently was clever enough; there were the howlers and squealers, those who took their cue from the first with fierce *éclats de rire* (only the French gives the thundering laughter its due), the walkers who couldn't sit still and manufactured reasons to march. "Miz Segal, I found a lunchbag on a floor. D'ya want it?" In fact, he was already at my desk with it. "It's mine, Miz Segal," Mary called out. "He took it from my pile under my desk. He's always snatchin' my stuff. Tell him to stop."

Now the exhibitionist and the howlers jump in with appropriate action, reducing the gentle girl to tears. She hadn't yet learned the laws of survival.

But in between the periods of horseplay we learned—they and I too. They were all academic—that is, college bound. When I asked at the beginning of the year who was planning to go to college, twenty hands went up. "Which colleges? For what careers?" One boy wanted to become a gym teacher so he could be a coach. One girl wanted to be a nurse. The rest would go to Bible college or business college. Others said they'd work a few years, then go. The goal was vague, the aspirations low because their need and expectation for achieving the goal was low. This mirrored the disbelief of their teachers and parents.

But the potential was there, even though the sophisticated language was not, and we had some exciting learning in that class and others like it using a technique I'd developed many years before.

At the beginning of the term we played a game called "The

The Challenge of E. Washington Rhodes

Round Table Open Talk Session." It was open talk but it wasn't round table. The seats and desks with their inkwells had been bolted irrevocably to the floor in 1912 in six parallel lines. The game consisted of the students presenting for consideration and study those topics which were of great importance to them. The same topics generally found themselves on the blackboard: civil rights, police, teen-age problems with all the subdivisions, sex, drinking, dating, parents, etc. Then we selected the four subject areas by vote, condensing many of the ideas under topical headings. The class divided into four groups, each going to a corner of the room. Each group selected its chairman and secretary. For two days the students read on their topic, brought the material to school for discussion by the group, and on the third day the secretary prepared the notes, which were presented to the entire class by the chairman. For several days thereafter, there were majority and minority reports, rebuttal and written expressions on the subjects.

It was a great game. The nine or so students in each group developed an easy relationship. They talked up a storm. Youngsters who had scarcely opened their mouths in class the first week were being active, vocal, militant, or sullen. But it was coming out. And from that time on it was their class; a free class, structured, controlled, but free in spirit.

One of my deepest convictions born of this game which I've played in class for twenty-five years is that, given the proper attitude and enthusiasm of the teacher and the proper preparation of the class, all students—star, average, slow—all, save mentally retarded children, are capable of academic education. This I believe is the birthright of each child: that he have a complete education composed of the multi-cultures of America. Together with this right each child should have exposure to the technical skills so that he might understand the dignity of labor and serve many of his own life needs.

I ought not to speak so glibly of mentally retarded children. Let it be recorded that the wealthiest society in the world has an infant population, black and white, born with visual-perceptual deficiencies. A Philadelphia psychiatrist has made a comprehensive study of these children and concludes that much of the mental retardation exhibited by them is correctable with simple, inexpensive methods in their early years. A lack of these corrections means permanent damage. While we allow the lack to exist, we condemn thousands of children to retardation.

Coming back to the effects of the Open Talk Groups in that 1961-62 year, Jimmy Wiggins was in my eleventh grade although he was old enough to be a senior. He came to school dressed well, was always on time, was respectful and quiet. He spoke rarely that first and second week. It was when he opened his mouth and when he walked with the hop and hip jerk that is the strut of the gang that I realized Jimmy was a part of the gangs. But there was a difference about him. One could tell immediately who in the classes were gang members. Maceo was the leader of the Morroccos (*sic*), Jason was a runner for the 56th Street gang. But Jimmy was different. Just how, we discovered at the end of the Round Table. He'd been elected chairman by his group, which was studying teen-age problems. At the end of three days Jimmy gave his report to the entire class. It was the consensus of his group that gangs were very destructive and should be eliminated, that the gang member had to lose every way, by injury or death, by imprisonment and thus destruction of oneself.

During the general question period a few members of the Lords, a gang just out of the territory, jeered at the statements in Jimmy's report. He didn't know what he was talking about.

"Don' I?" Jimmy asked calmly. "How come ya figger that?"

"Ya tryin' ta soun like ya in widda gang. We don' never see ya. Ya puttin' on. A gang is pertection. Nobody gawn bother us when we's together. We gawn beat'em all."

"You wrong," Jimmy answered quietly. "You not gawn win out over nobody. Ya gotta lose like I said, y'either gawna die or ya gawna be as good as dead when they finish widya in jail. I know. I just got outa Shelby school two months ago." Jimmy stopped to enjoy the gasp of astonishment and the open mouths. In one paragraph he had become a hero. I sat stunned by the news that he should have had this experience so early in his life. I was impressed by Jimmy's command of the class and their palpable respect for him.

"What ya git busted for?"

"For stealin' cars."

"How many ya steal?"

"Hundreds."

"Ya make a lota money?"

"Whattya think?"

"Ya dressin' boss!"

"Nah, my stepfather buy this when I come out."

"What happen to the money?"

"Gamble and lost it."

"Ya wuz jes' unlucky ya get busted and lose ya money. We ain't gettin' caught."

"You wrong. You all get caught. Anyhow when them jailbirds and proctors finish with ya, ya ain' good but for more crime ona outside."

"So how come ya in school?"

"I wuz lucky. A older proctor took a shine to me in Shelby. He tell me I look like his brother only nigger and he talk to me all'a time. We wuz real good friends a whole year. He watch me an' don't let the bigger boys do what they always do to the younger ones. And he give me books to read."

"So what? That mean ya gonna keep readin' now you're out? That's dumb!"

"Yeh, I'm gawna keep readin' and I'm gawna do what Al made me promise, to go back to school even if I'm two years older than the rest a'ya. He made me promise I'd try to get into a college an' my stepfather said he help. But don't none of you punks try ta tell me 'bout gangs and doin' time. I'm givin' ya the real thing. Git out while ya got ya life."

If the Round Table did nothing more all year, it had paid its way. It was a valuable lesson for the class. For me it was another example of readiness and one's moment of motivation, of the potential in each person, of what one human can and must mean to another.

A teacher without a sense of humor has a tough time in the classroom, especially in a ghetto school. His disaffection makes him a forbidding teacher and it's hard enough to pack in the subject matter without having to do it under very sober conditions.

I suppose one of the reasons I enjoyed being with a class was that fun was with people; in this case, young people. Overall, I have always enjoyed evoking a hearty and spontaneous laugh from an audience, and, after all, the class could be a good audience. A good teacher should also be a good ham. It seemed to me, too, over the years, that children of the poor and children of low- and middle-income minorities had a better-developed funny bone, which served them in difficult situations. The students who griped that they were in "drastic" arts, or the "epidemic" course, or in the "mortified" section were telling it on themselves. These were jokes they understood and laughed about because they had to live through these degrading conditions.

The small tragedies were as poignant as was the humor. They were part of life in 1961. Ronny was a slow student lost in an average class. But he was a fine young man, cooperative, trying hard, but not quite making it. His classmates were intolerant of his responses, which were never quite right, and Ronny felt the censure and disdain of his peers.

One day as I looked at student paintings being exhibited on the faculty room walls I peered, mouth agape, at the signature on a water color I was admiring. Tiny letters in the corner of the large painting said RONALD GASH, almost as if he had been ashamed to sign it. Was it my Ronald Gash? Could there be another in the school? I thought about the painting all day. It was lovely—an atelier-posed spread of fall flowers, wheat pods in a vase. Lying on the table before it was a fiddle with no strings. There was a feeling of the russet of Indian summer and the sonority of the violin in the rich mahogany of the instrument. I loved the painting and knew I had to have it. Ronny came into class at 1:45, and I couldn't restrain myself. But I was sorry the moment I opened my mouth, because I might be embarrassing him. Emotional people frequently move too hastily.

"Ronny, is that your painting in the faculty room?" He nodded, pleased, and I breathed with relief and pleasure.

"I want to talk to you after class."

I asked him if he wanted to sell the painting.

"Sell it?" he asked incredulously. "I'll give it to ya."

"No, I want you to talk to your art teacher. Ask her how much to charge me."

He returned the next day with a figure. His teacher said to charge me five dollars. He protested it was too much.

"Will you be satisfied, Ronny?"

"Satisfied? Ma'am! I don't wanna charge ya nothin'."

"You have to. When will I have it?"

"Soon as the exhibit's finished. In a week. 'N then I'll mat it for ya."

A week later Ronny came into the class carrying the painting to my desk. I stripped the paper away and was delighted with my purchase. As Ronny stood there, I quickly wrote out a check to Ronald Gash. I called the class to attention, showed them the painting, which was admired by all. I told them Ronald was the artist and that I had just bought it. With that I handed him the check. His brown skin blushed red with embarrassment, but the applause as he went to his seat had given him new stature. After class, he came to splutter some piece of joy that was bubbling in him. He seemed to have swelled with his new self-esteem, the most vital of personality needs.

"Ronnie," I asked, "why didn't your violin have strings?"

"Didn' know it had to."

"You never saw a violin?"

"My violin didn' have none when I foun' it."

"Where did you find it?"

"Miz Banks said to bring stuff from home fer a still life, 'n I didn' have nothin'. But on my way to school all'a trash was on'a pavements. That's where I found the violin, on'a trash."

"On'a trash" . . . The exceptional talent in the eye and hand of this sad, declassed young man; his sensitivity to beauty! "On'a trash" . . . So much tremendous talent being wasted in our land . . ."on'a trash."

It was just a coincidence that I happened to see and buy his painting. It was a coincidence that there was a Miss Janette Banks at West Philadelphia High, a lovely, black, young art teacher who knew talent, who gave inspiration and understood the need of this young man.

Ronald was given a scholarship to Moore College of Art even though he did not have an academic diploma. It didn't matter to Ronald if he didn't get a B.S. He became a fine artist, and a dignified man. The name of the game—dignity.

I had spent a year touching the lives of children who knew little of themselves and who had the lowest regard for their abilities. One floated along with the tide. And if the tide was too swift, if the tide threatened, one tried, feebly, to overcome the danger. But feebly. There was just too much tide; too much self-deprecation. Yet, the secret hope that is the nature of man remained buried deeply, a hope for revenge or self-advancement—but hope.

Lorenzo was a dull boy in a dull class that year. His was one of the 180 to 190 compositions I took home every Friday afternoon for marking. His compositions were always pedestrian, poor pieces of writing, no better than his taciturn, sullen speech. But this week Lorenzo had given me something vital. Thursday the class talked about civil rights—what were they and who had them. Lorenzo could not offer more than a vague, jumbled thought. He used the composition the next day to spill all the words he could not speak—hot, angry words, heartbroken feelings. He had done exactly what I urged. "Write down your thoughts. Just put down your thinking words, and these ideas will be your composition."

Lorenzo wrote about a dream he had had. He wrote it as a dream, but I knew this was merely a protective device for hostile thoughts:

All Negroes inhabited a distant planet and Lorenzo had never known any life other than that in this green and happy garden. Everyone had love and plenty to eat. There was no stealing or killing, because no one knew about things like that. Only the old grandmothers remembered that back on earth there had been people who were evil.

And then one day an amazing animal came out of the sky, settling down on their planet, and from its belly came ten men —at least the children who saw them thought they were men. It was just that they were bleached out and colorless. In fright the children ran to their homes to report the strange event. Lorenzo described the scene to his grandmother, who began to cry.

"Why are you crying, Grandmother?"

"Because evil is coming to our garden. You remember when you were small I told you how, on earth, the white men were our masters and worked us very hard, like animals. Then they freed us and we all shined white men's shoes until we hated ourselves and them. And there came a time when our hate toward each other made life too miserable. That's when all the Negroes came up here. Now it will start all over again." Lorenzo's grandmother rocked and cried.

"Grandmother," Lorenzo said, "don't cry. I'm going down where those pale men are and we'll capture them. Then we'll make shoe shiners of them and they will be our slaves."

Lorenzo's grandmother stopped crying and drew him to her.

"No, child, we will never do to them what they did to us. That way we will bring the terrible evil here to our green planet. We will welcome them to our good life and teach them love."

This was Lorenzo W.'s composition on that Friday in 1961 —mute, unbright, deprecated Lorenzo with a silent burning in his gut. The thoughts were there. All they needed was the readiness and the method of getting the words said.

Was it too late to provide a change agent for students in high school? Were their personalities set? We believed that given a motive, the goals and rewards, most humans can change all during life.

3

In the Beginning...

The Motivation Program was an idea whose time had come. It was an idea that had actually been born in the concern of the Government for the Soviets' superiority in space. Sputnik, in 1957, had thrown the country's planners and, through them, the educators into a spin. The trouble was, they said, that we weren't preparing enough kids to be scientists. This started a massive push across the country to saturate the *academically capable* with science and math so that we could compete with the Russians.

There was the rub: Who were the academically capable? In whom should the country put its hopes? And where were they to be found? The obvious answers were that our people were the greatest resource, but when respondents were questioned further, it appeared that by "our people" they meant the traditional groups of children who held high educational aspirations. Where were they? The poor blacks and Puerto Ricans had become the majority in the inner-city schools rather precipitously, and the better-prepared whites moved with their families to the outer-rim or suburban schools.

The solid black, inner schools now began to decline in teacher stability and in educational quality. As the blacks were ousted from ghettos that were being destroyed for redevelopment, the new density of student population was condensed into the schools just as their families were compressed into the new ghettos around the schools.

Where were the children who were to become the leaders, the intellectual leadership of the nation? Obviously they were not expected to come out of black schools—well, rarely, at any rate. In those days, one still spoke of Negroes. These were the years before one's blackness was a thing to be proud of. The educated leadership was to come out of the white society. Only sporadically did one find small pockets where a fearless teacher or principal risked laughter by wanting to upgrade the education of his Negro students.

Across the city, Dr. Ruth Hayre at William Penn High School and Martin Rosenberg at Benjamin Franklin High School took these risks with two of the earliest attempts in the nation to upgrade and enrich the education of Negroes. I became familiar with these programs when, as the appointee charged with formulating a program for West Philadelphia High School, I went to see what was being done with limited funds in these schools. The two schools had become sad ghosts of once-proud educational institutions. I looked, too, at the Higher Horizons Program in New York. Each had interesting features, but I was not content with the composite.

Many people were setting these new goals. There was no doubt that the questions posed by Eugene Washington Rhodes were becoming matters of prime importance. At West Philadelphia High, Jack Neulight, the principal, initiated weekly seminars to discuss the problems of the school. One of the serious shortcomings, we decided, was that the academic life of the school had become nil. Gone were the scholarship awards, as Mr. Rhodes had shown at the beginning of the year; gone were the great numbers of students applying and being accepted into colleges. Academic life had indeed become less than mediocre and depressing. The capable children were not coming to West Philadelphia High. This is not to say that there weren't exciting master teachers stimulating, plugging away, caring about the children. Si Richardson, Bess Abramowitz, Cornie Stephens, Bernie Ivens, Alice Graham, Tom Campbell, Helen Ansley, Isadore Klingsberg, John French, Betty Davis, Carolyn and Wendell Pritchett, Frances Austin, Hank Weisberg are a very few of many teachers who did not lose heart or allow their standards to fall. But the tone of the whole school had slipped fairly close to rock bottom.

During the year of thinking, meeting, and talking, Helen Ansley, the social studies head, invited students to join a group who would tour the University of Pennsylvania for three days. Sixty students, some in academic courses, many taking advantage of three days out of school for the lark, opted for the experience. Some of these were my own students.

Gathering the results of the talking, the bits of programs tried and observed, and adding my own varied experiences, I set out in the summer of 1962 to construct a proposal for presentation to the principal and his cabinet in the fall.

The Motivation Program of West Philadelphia High School wasn't born of fantasy. On the contrary it came out of the need of the times, out of hundreds of live experiences, mine and those of other teachers who felt that it was time to give kids a break. All of us had observed human behavior and travail for a lifetime and we'd begun to formulate a philosophy. It was at this point in late 1962 that the goals of the "M" Program were enunciated. All summer I hammered out my own ideas and what I believed to be those of my associates at West Philadelphia High School and also of Leo Molinaro (executive vice-president of The West Philadelphia Corporation, a subsidiary of the University of Pennsylvania, and my friend) and officials of the three universities of University City. Thus, we codified our credo and our goals:

Credo

Each man, irrespective of religion, race, or ethnic origin, is a powerhouse of creative strength. This strength, fully developed, will mean vitality to him, to the community, and to the American people.

We believe that many human beings do consider themselves of low ability and therefore develop little need for achievement. Thus, much power is lost. We believe that the individual, convinced of his ability to succeed in a goal within his grasp, will embrace more readily varied educational opportunities and will strive toward his goal.

The Motivation Program of West Philadelphia High School believes that a vast number of students with excellent potential for higher education are lost each year because they have not believed themselves capable, nor has college been a believable goal. The purpose of the program is to seek out and to develop those students with hidden potential for higher education, those with poor achievement, as well as those who compete easily for marks, but are unmotivated to strive for their best. The success of the program is measurable by the student's developing pride in self, in his need to achieve and in the setting of goals for the future.

How are these desirable ends achieved? What ingredients are contained in this program to see the "moment of motivation," the readiness for each student? Which teacher, which neighbor, which circumstance touches his life or hers and opens for him new and brighter horizons? The "M" Program is composed of four fundamental parts of a coherent program designed to enrich, broaden, and motivate the selected students. These are curricular enrichment, parent and community involvement, cultural enrichment, and tutoring.

Goal

This is the Motivation Program. It is a program in which we, the home, school and total community, join to develop the vast reservoir of power in our midst: the human mind and spirit. It is our hope that this belief and participation will bring about the greatest fulfillment of our young people.

As I read back over each sentence I'd written, its pompous quality annoyed me. It sounded so "elevated" in tone; so very "intellectual." I started over, trying to put my meaning into plainer prose. No matter how I amended, it came out the same way. Finally the realization of what I was saying became quite evident to me: The thought, the concept, the regard for the human being and his potential was indeed a larger-than-life view and could not be reduced to mean language. I realized that my own concern with how my feelings were coming out in ink were a direct reflection of how my society feels about fellow humans, their talents and place in life. How else, then, could one utter these grandiose ideas?

Well, if that was the answer to my perplexity, I decided I would have to tolerate the cynics, the discriminators, yes, and the racists, while we went about proving our philosophies. Years later, it seems almost incredible that there should have been as much resistance to the basic credo as we met. But there it was. We saturated the community, business and intellectual, around the school—that is, University City. We were uttering heresies about human potential, general educational abilities and capabilities of all people. The group most difficult to convince were teachers (though not all). Many at West Philadelphia were and remain exciting, progressive educators who believed in people and who had not given up growing and maturing themselves. It is due to these people together with the administration, the parents, and the community that the credo, the goals, the aspirations, took on the flesh of human beings.

The simplest part of the preparation, that summer of 1962, was the thinking and writing up of proposals and program, even though the summer work itself had been an all-consuming task while I was going through it. The major task was yet to come. I armed myself with the program, which had been endorsed by the principal and cabinet, and a set of promotional procedures I felt the program would need if it were to have a chance of success. With these I set off through the school to address the tenth-grade academic sections. I planned to describe to them what we had in mind. Remembering well the

In the Beginning . . .

apathy and disinterest in academic matters which I'd seen displayed in the Rhodes assembly, the year before, I expected my presentation to be greeted by silence or, at best, some tepid questions.

My appeal to the students was along the same lines as the proposal I had prepared. I used the urgency our Government was displaying in having fallen behind the Soviet in the race for space. I told them of our beliefs that all humans have great potential which is not used; that we in West Philadelphia had been given an opportunity of proving our theories. We believed we could and that we would achieve certain goals if we would all work together toward that end.

I described the program; all students selected would have to give us an additional hour a day because they would have to add a class in developmental English and one in a special math; all their other subjects would be enriched, therefore demanding more thought and more work. Tutoring would be available for emergency needs. I described the cultural program. Each student would be expected to attend at least two cultural activities a month and these events would be a cross section of the varied ethnic cultures of our own society. We would take trips in and out of the city. I felt a spark of interest. "To New York?" "Yes, among many other places." There would be one-, two- and three-day visits to the University of Pennsylvania, Drexel University (then Drexel Institute of Technology) and Philadelphia College of Pharmacy and Science, our neighborhood colleges, which they would be able to attend over an extended period. So far, at least, I had the attention of most of the students.

I had expected, unreasonably, that I would be seeing a gleam of excitement in their eyes. If I felt that way about what I was describing, why shouldn't they? It didn't happen. I became anxious. Where was this selling ability I thought I had? I continued developing my plan. Their parents would have to become an active part of the program. A loud groan greeted this announcement. I'd touched a nerve, evidently. Count down.

Further, I told them they would have more counseling and guidance than usual. A laugh, out loud. All these activities we believed would make them ready for college and help them develop their potential. Were there any questions? One girl asked when it would start. February, I responded. Another asked whether she could get out of the program if she didn't like it. I told them honestly that they would have to remain in the program until June because their rosters would have been arranged that way. There were a few heads wagging no. I was losing the game if the few vocal ones started a wave of disinterest.

"There is one important thing I should tell you, now," I said to them. It was a long chance. "Not everyone in these academic classes will be invited into the program. Not at the beginning, that is. I will do a study of your records and if your scores fit the criteria we've set, you'll be notified."

Half the class raised their hands, suddenly. "What do you mean by criteria?" I explained that their reading and math scores would have to be at least eighth-grade level now that they were in the tenth grade. They couldn't be more than two years behind to be able to catch up. Then they would have to go to Drexel University for a battery of tests. Only then would they be told whether or not they are to be included in the program.

Many hands popped up, now. "What can we study for the examination? How will we get ready for it?"

"There will be no way to study," I answered. "This will be a test of how much you have learned since first grade and how well you understand your reading, but if you don't make it this time, perhaps it will be possible next year."

Now every hand was in the air. I felt a sudden anxiety in their sounds. *If you don't make it!* That was it. I realized the moment I said the words that I had made bingo. The answer to my next question told me for sure. "How many of you think you would like to participate in the program *if you are selected?*" All hands in the room went up. I knew that was the answer. They had reacted like all people no matter what the age or activity. The fact that they were to be selected as a special group made it desirable. It was a positive and gigantic step we had taken that day. That was the initial step needed to enhance their self-esteem, to make them see themselves differently from their past image. It was part of our stock, our goal and our philosophy although it was not yet salable to all my associates at that time. I felt that although motivation had to be inspired from exterior forces, it was the condition in the personality, the seedbed of one's image, which either propelled or retarded effective movement. This was an old philosophy. The dignity and centrality of the self was taught by the earliest Chinese philosophers. "A man must not lose face." The Bible taught that if you humiliate a man, you destroy him. Conversely, to nourish his self-esteem, to instill belief in himself is to provide man with mobility and a need to develop his natural greatness.

The testing of 135 tenth-grade students in the academic portion of the class was undertaken by the psychological testing department at Drexel for that first year. The criteria established for the program used a minimum of eighth-year math and reading with the tenth-grade students' level, since financial considerations dictated some boundaries. Boundaries are hurtful to people, but they are society's realities. When the scores were reviewed the testers left me with their conviction that most of these students tested would never make it into college; they had neither language nor mathematical skill; their IQ's were low; they were not college material and the program was starting with a real handicap. I'd heard such sentiments many times, all over the world, from sundry authorities whose weighty judgments determined others' lives. I'd pored over the "iron lung," which was the repository in each school organization room of the vital statistics of each student; when I say vital statistics, I mean it. These graphs and these numbers were the stuff which followed a student through his school career and which determined his future life, his success. This iron-bound book—iron-bound in more than name, for these records were destined for professional eyes only—was a source of wonder for me. Someone would have to give me an answer to my constant question: How come in instance after instance the students had registered 112, 115, 122, 108, 105 IQ in the second-grade testing, falling six to eight points by the fifth grade and another ten to fifteen points by the eighth grade? Could it be that many people develop into high-grade imbeciles the farther they go in school? Was this a logical assumption? What was the relationship of frequent lateness and absence to low IQ or low reading level? The children with many absences showed up poorly in the tests and on the graphs of the "lung," which followed them from school to school, teacher to teacher, influencing their opinions. A priori, these records set the stage again for failure as teacher and student were programmed by records.

Despite these limitations, in this first Motivation class, which would be graduated in 1965, we didn't have the heart to turn away many of the kids whose criteria didn't measure up. Most of the students had very low IQ's. At least that's what the "lung" and Drexel said. But frequently in the records, there was some small sign that the low IQ didn't tell the whole story. Then, I'd talk to junior high counselors and teachers. There were many generous people who said, "Try that student."

We'd see what we could do with youngsters who had been sold a bill of goods. And that's what we began doing. Every day, in every class, on every trip, with every parent, with every community friend, we worked to change the "M" student's image of himself, to help him understand his worth, to *him* and to *us*.

There was an instance two years later when the school "M" advisory group evaluated our progress. One teacher of an "M" class and a counselor with problems in her recent marriage, but both with disdain and dislike for blacks (and average whites, too), spoke up about the arrogance of the "M" '65 class. "They all have swelled heads about themselves!"

It wasn't a new bit of information. I saw it happening in a

few cases. As I met day after day with each of the hundreds of "M." students, I saw a marked metamorphosis in some girls and boys. These were gulping in my propaganda and were getting indigestion in the swallows. The majority, however, were moving from unbearable diffidence and self-deprecation to articulate confidence. I wasn't concerned about this criticism. The children would level off as they understood themselves and their society better. I learned from incidents such as these what was to be confirmed years later in a film called *The Victims*, made by Dr. Spock—that there were two victims of prejudice, those who received the wound and those who gave it.

Back to the testing. I've kept several hundred of those Drexel test record charts of three Motivation classes. They are very human accounts to me, for they exhibit how little we know about the mind, the spirit, and the will to achieve.

Here are a few samples of how they showed in 1963 and 1964, their tenth and eleventh years, and where they are now. The IQ is the combination of verbal and nonverbal scores of the California Mental Maturity tests. With a 115 IQ as the widely accepted score for academic children who wanted to go to college or at least to enter a good academic high school of our city, the scores below did indeed seem impossible ones to overcome.

NAME	COMBINED IQ	STATUS–1971
Martha B.	89	Teacher, elementary school
Clara S.	96	Student, doctoral program for educational administration
Jessie T.	110	Teacher, elementary school
Harold C.	101	Student, medical school
James C.	91	Electronics engineer
Sheryl F.	101	English teacher, "M" class

NAME	COMBINED IQ	STATUS–1971
Francis R.	100	Third-year student, law school
Sara C.	97	College senior
Cal S.	84	Second-year student, law school
Sheila R.	94	Teacher, elementary school
Mel T.	102	Student, doctoral program in psychology

I have selected for demonstration those students whose IQ's were low. There were some fairly high IQ's, 120-139. One young man hit 145. But the motivation problems were the same for these as well as the students who tested low. They all felt less than worthy, uncared for, incapable, and hopeless. Their output, their desire to learn showed this clearly. Every day brings me confirmation that, given the motivation, most can achieve the goal they set.

In my final talk to "M" students of one of the summer programs, I invited the students to come to me for help at any time and with any need. This included during high school, college, or when they were ready for a job.

Cynthia called me on Saturday, February 5, 1972. "Mrs. Segal, you said to call you when we needed help. I'm graduating in June and I need a teaching job!" Cynthia was one of the least likely to succeed. And she made her goal. Who is to judge?

A few weeks ago I attended a concert at which the soloist was a West Philadelphia High School, "M" '67 graduate.

As a student, Norman Eric Johns had played in the West Philadelphia High Orchestra. Who could have foretold that this student who liked the cello would one day be a student of the world-famous Elsa Hilger? After the excellently performed concert I spoke with Miss Hilger. She expressed great hopes for the professional future of this young man. She told me that she had been willed a fine cello to be granted to an exceptional student, and that she had presented it to him.

"The day I gave him the cello," Miss Hilger said, "he carried it home and stayed up until three A.M. making music on this wonderful instrument." Another sweet success—and riches for our cultural life.

We sought continuously to find techniques that might provide pleasure, enhancement of self-esteem, and simply a reward for a task or a step well done. The enrichment classes, trips, cultural experiences, Host Visits, University College co-op classes, seminars, Open Talk Groups, law classes, St. Joseph's College chemistry courses—every activity was photographed. This testimony to the "M" students' commitment went up on the "M" office bulletin boards.

Each March a huge board went up. Photos and names of colleges to which the "M" students will go covered the board. Each year the board was made larger.

At the end of the school year a festive "M" evening was held for students, parents, and the incoming tenth-grade "M" students and their parents. At this time students performed and received awards for the greatest attendance at concert, opera, theater, Host Visit, etc.

At St. Joseph's College advanced credit chemistry course graduation, each "M" student is presented with a citation for special achievement, which goes to the college with his transcript for the advanced college credit.

Finally, all "M" students receive a citation of achievement, which goes to the colleges. Every reward, written, oral, or tangible, has its meaning and the end result is the achievement of the goals.

> The support making the most impression on the student is that of his parents. It is the quality of their regard, the delicate, emotional relationship, that arms the young with a need to please and a will to achieve.

4
Bridging the Generation Gap

All the techniques for stimulation described in the previous pages were built into the Motivation Program as it started with the first 135 tenth-grade girls and boys, twenty of whom were ostensibly "star" pupils because they could pull down one or two A's in the majors. All of them, every one, from my point of view, had been undereducated, shortchanged, in their elementary and junior high schools. All, including the stars, were apathetic. There was no aspiration. This new program for which the youngsters had volunteered was not compensatory but a recognition of where they were now and the setting of almost unrealistic goals for all of their academic work. Their volunteering meant that they would meet us halfway and undertake more and more difficult work and classes, be willing to be guided to every kind of academic, cultural, and social experience. By joining the program the students were pledging their cooperation, their good behavior, and their willingness to become partners in the future. They and the parents agreed to this. By February 1, the "M" students moved into their new rosters with ten periods of English and eight in math each week. Part of the work was in the traditional curriculum and part in developmental areas of literature, creative writing, logic and mathematical concepts. For a few periods each week over the next two years the special motivation English and math teachers provided the "M" students with compensatory English and math, concepts and drill that would help them compete in the springboard to college—the college board examination. This was the additional work they undertook willingly, not as a crash program but as a long range enrichment in two vital areas. The math head, Isadore Klingsberg, and the English head, Hank Weisberg, with the approval of our Principal Jack Neulight, made available additional teacher time and planned with us the kind of enrichment we wanted. Elizabeth Davis and Bess Abramovitz, two creative science teachers who had studied a new BSCS (Biological Sciences Curriculum Series) genetic approach to biology, threw themselves excitedly into what everyone said was way beyond what "these students" could understand, and each year thereafter they moved from the yellow, to the green, to the blue versions, each more difficult than the last course, proving that their belief in the students was not misplaced.

We invited the community to help us. Dr. James Nixon, an orthopedist with the Veterans Hospital and physician to the Eagles football team, came in to lecture to the science classes and contributed a fully articulated skeleton to the program. Dr. Pinchas Shub, a University of Pennsylvania mathematician, an elderly, charming man, came out of his ivory tower to talk math to our young people, captivating the young "M" students.

We used the February term to get our feet wet, to make the model, the structure around which we could build and make changes as we saw the need.

There were two advisory committees that worked with us. One was composed of a cross section of teachers and vice-principals at West Philadelphia High. The other was made up of the vice-presidents of the colleges of University City. This committee, which met each month, came prepared to listen to my plans, to suggest, and to make available whatever I felt necessary.

Leo Molinaro, executive vice-president of The West Philadelphia Corporation and my next-door neighbor, has one of the most fertile and exciting imaginations I have ever encountered, and every idea I brought to the meeting became the core of a vital new project. He brought with him the power of Dr. Gaylord Harnwell, president of the University of Pennsylvania and president, also, of the Corporation. Dr. Harnwell, physicist, teacher, humanist, was taken by the enthusiasm and conviction of Leo Molinaro and myself. He made available the facilities and services of the University. He encouraged professorial and administrative staff to participate. His appearances at our functions reinforced the esteem we were fostering and his offer of great scholarship help to our "M" grads gave the Motivation Program solidity as an honest and total package.

That first year, I suggested that each "M" class should have an induction ceremony for both students and their parents at which time the students would make their commitment to the program and to themselves. It was Leo who said, "Let's give them a gold pin with an "M" on it at the ceremony." He provided us with them, and each year at the induction event, each "M" class pinned on the gold "M" in a spirit of affirmation. No matter how it was explained, it was difficult for some teachers to understand that this was not a "reward for nonaccomplishment" but rather a designation by one who had taken on new responsibility; that it would serve as a daily reminder and a spur. Even so, that half-inch gilt pin rankled in some teachers' puritanical pedagogical craws.

I saw what this golden circle meant in the life of one child that summer of 1963. One day during the hot summer, I drove through the sad destruction of the Mantua neighborhood, utter desolation. There were gaping lots filled with rubble, the playground for children and rats. There, sitting on a broken step, was a girl. From the car my eye caught the gleam of a gold circle on a collar. Then quickly I took in the picture. There was my "M" student, Bernetha, sitting amid her poverty, her sole adornment the gold pin, and in her hands one of the ten books I had assigned. I called out, "Bernetha," in friendship. She looked up, surprised with my sudden appearance, embarrassed by her clothes. She pointed excitedly to her pin. Why had she been moved in that small moment to think of her pin, of its importance to her? The pin was a symbol of what had begun happening to her. She would be someone in her dreams. Bernetha was one of the thousands of "M" students in these intervening years who have been stirred by this new ingredient, an appreciation of self. Today she is transferring this quality to her second-grade students.

I was filled with exciting plans for the full year of the "M" Program which began in September. A foundation had read our proposal and goals and was impressed enough to give us a two-year, $50,000 grant starting in September. What a bonanza! Richard Bennett, the sensitive, sophisticated man who directed the foundation, was encouraging and most agreeable to ideas. So the whole world was possible for us in that year.

One of the first problems, I saw, was that the stutents were reading only three books a year and writing a composition once a month, if that. This wasn't the quality of English course our students needed. I would help bring about change in these areas together with cooperative teachers and Hank Weisberg, hoping it would get our students ready for college. As a test project, therefore, I compiled a book list with small descriptive blurbs of seventy great books. I gave the first motivation class, "M" '65, an assignment before school was out in June. Each one was to select ten books, read them and write a book report on each. These would be due in September. There was anger and open hostility at the June "M" students meeting. There was only one "M" group in the school that first year. They resented the assignment, it was unfair, it would spoil their summer vacation, etc. My response, as we discussed the matter openly, was that these were books they would need in college, and if they didn't use the summers for some of the books, they would not get hooked on reading. This was my goal. I'd had calls from many parents. Most were pleased with my demands. Some felt I was being too demanding. My last word to the students was that it was a voluntary effort. They didn't have to do it. But then I added a reward. I promised that their reports would be passed on for credit to their eleventh-year English teachers. The reward was important.

From 135 students I received 1,110 book reports, which I read, commented upon, and passed to the teachers. Some students refused the assignment. Today, eight years later, those first students still comment on the many values they derived from that first discipline.

When the Motivation Program began, one of our problems was to hammer out our philosophy about motivation and then set about making change. I concluded that self-esteem was a vital ingredient in a person's makeup. I believed it existed to greater or lesser degree in all personalities and that outside forces could be the stimulus or the depressant for this personality factor.

The parents, therefore, became a primary factor in the stimulus. They had to be amendable to change of various kinds because the problems were varied among children. Although the majority were black, there was nevertheless a group of whites. Not all blacks were poverty level; not all whites were middle class. But they had certain similarities. They were all bright, they were all underproducing and they were willing to play along with me as I handed out huge doses of convincing promotion to them and their parents about their unused ability and their potential for college.

It was this promotion, I believe, that built up the determination and the goals in students. But it could not have been done with students alone. The parents had to feel that way about themselves for it to rub off on the children. I brought to the new program a belief born of experience that parents wanted the best for their children; that if they are convinced the goals are achievable they will become active partners in the work. Convincing the "M" parents, therefore, of the achievability of the goals inspired in them aspirations for their children that were an immediate spur for everyone in the home, including the adults themselves. But how could we translate the goals into action? Would communication between the two make the bridge?

One boiling hot Sunday in June, 250 Motivation parents came to a career conference. A conference chairman who was the vice-president of a university and ten workshop chairmen who were top professionals in their fields worked closely with our parents. Already normally concerned parents, they returned home more knowledgeable and with new hopes and possibilities for themselves and their children. The conference had provided an instrument for communication between the generations and one to enhance the self-esteem of the adults, a quality needed by all of us as we grow mature.

The monthly Motivation Parents Group provided as much inspiration and motivation for me as it did for them. From the beginning I had been fortunate enough to convince many of the "M" parents of my sincerity and my overriding determination to help their children. They believed in me and stood with me even against some negative blacks.

In the last decade, we have been made captive by cynical people, whites and blacks who have gained personally by deprecating their own ethnic group, or another. They've sown discord in the name of "the community" and they've planted fear of each other when each should have believed in the other. There are those blacks who consider suspect any white who has thrown in his life with the black community. Thus my application, my total immersion in this program, this philosophy I believed in, provided a temporary hate platform for a black politician, whose star, happily, has since been eclipsed.

The "M" Parents Group that month had invited a psychiatrist to address them after we'd worked through an hour of problems pertaining to the "M" students. As I sat behind the speaker on the platform, I became aware of some disturbance outside the auditorium doors. It was later, during the socializing, that a parent related the cause of the noise.

A misanthropic black politician had stopped in to listen. He'd heard about some sh-- being fed Negroes in here. "What's all this motivation crap they're being brainwashed with? They don't even know what the word means. They're being bought with coffee and cake!" And more of the same. It was one of the parents, a devoted father, who invited the demagogue to sit down and shut up or get out. This was the last time we were bothered. The parents had begun seeing the Program as theirs and weren't about to let it be harmed.

Parents are sad people. Often they have little to be glad about. And mostly, people have more sadness than gladness. But they have to have hope every step of the way or life becomes an impossible burden.

The parents who have had the good fortune of seeing their children through adolescence into the safety of adulthood and marriage with no unhappy incidents to mar the scene are either remarkably wise and skillful parents or very lucky. Frequently the same wise and skillful upbringing by the same parents results in a series of escapades in a second child which produce early gray hair. Something obviously was different with the pattern. Often the parents self-righteously judge the failures of someone else's child from their successful position. None of it holds water and no one knows the answers. Much of what happens to a child is traceable to the early childhood training, his personality development plus the chance meetings and friendships with sundry other personalities and the chemistry involved. Many varieties of inputs have converged to determine the child's direction in the difficult journey through the forest of life, to use the Red Ridinghood allegory.

Low-income families, white, black, all ethnic groups, seem to have a tougher time showing their skill as parents. Many negative social factors militate against them. Nonetheless they continue struggling against an increasingly strong tide of society's malaise, hoping that their children, living in crowded conditions, getting the inferior education inherent in *de facto* segregated schools will, nevertheless, make it. But making it in those early days was very often a passive hope with little one could do to effect change. Today the middle- and high-income parents suffer the same problems with their children's social relationships. There are national and indeed international problems that reflect on the lives of all children, no matter what the economic status. The most serious problem we all felt was that parents and children weren't communicating. They were living together but talking by each other and if, as happened a few years later, one cannot talk to one's parents, if there is strife in the home with no plan for resolution, what is to happen? And when a catastrophe occurs, with whom are we to communicate? The Open Talk Sessions were among the "M" Program's most valuable projects to help create a bridge to each other.

This came to us forcefully during the calamitous weekend of Martin Luther King's assassination. Grief is an intimate pain; it is felt deeply in the core of oneself. Yet, the pain of Dr. King's murder was shared intimately by millions of wounded human beings. Each expressed the torment in his own way. The officials in high places convened hurriedly to prepare for the outbreak of civil hostilities across the country. The black leadership, each with a following, a philosophy, and program, though unorganized, unaligned, splintered, met immediately, and with urgency anticipating a great uprising. Big men, strong males, wept tears of anguish, of loss, as they realized the implications of the tragedy.

The black world stopped that Friday. The white world held its breath. No one came to school; what was the use, what for, if this could happen because a man was black. Only it had happened to John and Medgar. The kids were wild—even the "M" kids who were talking about things constantly with parents, with hosts, teachers, peers.

Saturday morning, as it happened, was the last of the seven sessions of the continuous Open Talk Groups of "M" students and their parents. The white kids were scared, but they came, impelled by a need to share the pain and fear.

Dr. Ruth Middleman and Thomas Pierce were the psychologists conducting this group of sessions with "M" students and parents. They met each week in rooms at the University of Pennsylvania.

Ruth telephoned Tom on Friday to ask his plans and his advice. Did he intend going to the session tomorrow? Would people come? She was as distraught as he. Should she come or would it add fuel to their anger? Tom, an "M" parent, an involved black, felt they had to face the kids together, the Jewish woman and the "black old man who had made their lousy world what it was."

For four hours on Saturday the Open Talk Session continued. No one went for a break, a lunch, or a smoke. The parents sat stonily. What could they say to help? Better to let the professionals handle the children.

"They killed him, Tom! How can you sit here for two hours and try to con us into coolin' it?"

"I'm tellin' you, Paul, over an' over. Ya gotta look at this thing with a cool eye."

"How can we, Tom? Just tell us how? We finally get us a leader and they kill 'im. Will we ever have another Martin? Tell me that, Tom. I can't stand it. I wanta go out and get every whitey I see!"

"And what'll that get ya, Roslyn?"

"Don't ask what it'll get her! Just because you're a psychologist you're gettin' a holy attitude. Don't forget you're a nigger too, like us, and if you don't get'em first they'll get you like they got Martin!"

"Yeah, Jim. I know how this is gettin' to you, but ya gotta ask yourselves why this tragedy happened and what we can do so he didn't die for nothin'."

"I don't care what you say; Martin Luther King died for nothin'. Whitey's always saying, 'Trouble with the Negroes is they don't have any leaders.' So we get a powerful leader and they kill'im."

"Dr. Middleman, I'm sorry you're here today. It's not a good day for blacks and whites to be together. O.K., Tom, you say,

'Ask why the tragedy happened'! You tell us, if you know all the answers!"

"But that's the point, kids. I don't know the answers, and Dr. Middleman and I are not with the twenty-eight of you to tell you answers. Goddamit. My generation sure doesn't know answers—we made all the mess."

"So how come you old ones always get on our backs telling us what to do and what not to do and what we gotta do?"

"That's part of the trouble with gettin' old, kids. We think we own the world and we know all the answers. But we don't. Sometimes you kids know more than we do. And that's what we're here for in these Open Talk Sessions every Saturday. We want to exchange ideas, kids and parents. We don't want you necessarily to accept the opinions or solutions the adults give you."

"Yeah, you want our opinions, just talk, talk. Sure, you're not tellin' us what to do or not do, oh no! But you're tellin' us to consider and think and figure it out and cool it! Cool it! We want to burn it, not cool it!"

"And we don't want any honkies here. Why's she here, Tom? It was O.K. for Dr. Middleman to be here the last six weeks, but no more! Not after Martin's murder Thursday night! Why did you come? We don't need any Jew liberal whiteys. Who asked for you?"

"I did, kids, and take it easy," Tom urged.

"Why, Tom? This is our time, it's our funeral, we don't need whitey liberals."

"But that's the point, isn't it? Isn't this why we come together to talk?—white, black, Jewish, Christian? To reason?"

"Ain't no time for reason, Tom. No more. Dr. Middleman, you're brave, comin' today. You shoulda stayed home and hid under the bed because the blacks see red today instead'a white. Why didya come, anyway? Just to rub our noses in the sh--?"

"Paul, I came because I had to, because my life is committed to people and people's feelings. So how could I have suddenly become unconcerned in the face of such a tragedy?"

"It's not your tragedy. It's ours. Don't take this from us too. You took everything for three hundred years, ya made us believe we were nothin'. Just leave us with our hero."

"Paul, Paul, wait! It isn't your tragedy alone. I want to claim some of it. How can it be yours and not mine if you and I are part of this country, if our future is tied up with each other?"

"Yeah, that's what the liberals all say only until they have to share—then they get just as greedy."

"No, Paul, don't dirty the word 'liberal.' Don't fall in the trap the haters are preparing for all of us. The liberals all through history got bloody getting an even break for humans. Remember that the slave underground railroad was made possible by the liberals."

"So how come they run out on us when the going is rough?"

"They don't, Paul, most of them stay with the fight. Some fall away because they're offended by irresponsible statements and bigotry from black members. It has to work from both ends. But I had to come, Paul. I have a stake here today."

"O.K., but if you get killed goin' home we won't be surprised. You're dumb to show yourself today."

"All right, I'm sorry if you feel that way. I have two teen-age boys and I'd like to be with them until they're grown and on their own. But if I have to die in this struggle, well that's how it is. I'm ready."

"Listen, kids, when Dr. Middleman called to talk about the assassination and about today, I agreed with her that we needed her here, to get with it, to be a part of us. If we're gawna help ourselves out of our mess we gotta value each other."

"Aah! there you go—we gotta value. Always us. Why don't they value? Did they ever care about our value?"

"Right, Bob. Are you saying then that the only way to teach them our value is to go out and burn? You want to kill them. How? In a riot? I know how bitter you are. So am I. But what will killing and burning accomplish?"

"Nothin'! But goddamit, we'll teach'em a lesson!"

"Only them? Do you think we can keep clear of the destruction? As always we'll end up sufferin' most."

"I don't care! If I'm gawna get caught in it, O.K., but I'll pull-'em down with me."

"You don't care about self-destruction? And do you think we can win even if we burn down five blocks, twenty blocks, ten miles? It's just a temporary inconvenience for them. Don't you see, kids, that this is what the whites need as an instrument for real serious repression? And if you think we've been behind the eight ball, just watch and see what the yahoos do. What do you think of that, Paul?"

"I won't listen, Tom. Your generation has tried it your way long enough. You're failures. You let'em crap on you and you loved it. We don't! And we won't! We'll show the bastard white livers what hate means!"

"Yeh! That's the only thing whites understand. When it hurts them in their pocketbook or scares the hell out of them."

"But, Sam, you're uptight about Martin's death and you wanna go out and burn, but he would tell you, 'No! That's not the way to win.' He'd say, 'That's a losing hand.' What about that?"

"Well, that's one part of him. I never took that nonviolent stuff. Where did it get him? Huh? Dead! real, nonviolent dead!"

"And who killed him? A white bastard. Always it's a white man who does it to us. I can't stand it anymore, I hate'em all. All of'em! I wanna kill'em all!"

Paul had voiced his fierce resentment and his pent-up anger directly at Dr. Middleman. She shriveled somewhat in her chair almost as if blistered by the heat of Paul's attack.

"Paul," she said quietly, "I don't blame you, all of you, for how you feel about whites. But I am asking you—you know me now. We're not all the same. Give those of us who have invested our lives in yours a chance, won't you?"

"No, no! I'll never get over my feeling about you."

"And don't expect any of us to save you when the revolution comes!" Bob shouted.

"We give up on you! Nothing'll ever change you. You're lousy, evil people. You're defective!"

"O.K., Greg"—Tom's strong voice stepped in—"they're

evil. But I want to give you a test case. I want to make a personal case of it. If I were walkin' down the street with her and a coupla blacks came up and tried to grease her, what should I do? Ditch her or go down with her?"

"Ditch her!"

"Leave her and run!"

"The hell with her!"

"She wouldn't save you if the case was turned around!"

"Why not?" Tom asked?

"She wouldn't take you to her house!"

"How do you know I wouldn't? I have black friends who are a very important part of my private life!" Dr. Middleman offered.

"Sure! To show off! Show niggers! That's what they are!"

"No, Paul, don't accuse me of such shallowness."

"Yeh! I know whites. You're all the same! You make me sick and I wanna puke when I'm with ya!"

"Paul, wait a minute." Tom Pierce touched Paul's arm. "Ya know I'm with you. We've reached an important point in today's talk. We'll never have another time together this important. And I'm gawna reach down with you to where you hurt and you're gawna level with me. Just cool it a few minutes. A few of you have told me in the last few weeks that all of you in the 'M' Program have a little different feeling about the whites in your class. You feel the fact that they wanted to stay at West to be in the Program meant to you that they had no hatred toward you. Am I right? Isn't this about what you were handing me before the murder? O.K., you're all pretty much agreeing to that. Now I don't know how close any of you feel to a white so I can't get personal with most of ya. But you, Paul. I'm gonna lay it to you. I know how close you and Mickey Cohen are. He's your buddy—you told the group a thousand times. He's Jewish, white, middle class, liberal, everything we're screamin' about today in our anger and frustration. O.K. I'm givin' you the case. We're in a riot on Lancaster Avenue. It can happen. You're walkin' with Mickey and a gang of blacks attack. What're you gawna do?"

"What d'ya think I'm gawna do?"

"Come on, quit stallin', Paul. The six guys are gawna grease Mickey. What're you gawna do? Will you desert him?" A chorus shouted its answer.

"Wait, I want Paul's answer."

"Aah, lay off, Tom. Why do you have to personalize it?"

"But that's what's important today, Paul. This whole thing is about people, individuals—the Pauls, the Mickeys, the Bobs, white, black, but individuals. So answer me. Will you desert Mickey?"

"He'll have to take his chances."

"Do you mean it, Paul? Why do you look so unhappy? Why are you so confused?"

"Christ, Tom, could I do it and feel good? I'll wanta kill myself if I desert him. He's the only white whose skin color I don't see. But we can't help it. We're in war. I can't answer. Tom, don't push me. I can't make my decision this minute! But, Dr. Middleman, you can tell your white friends we're sick and tired of hearing that prejudice is a disease, blah, blah. We don't care that the white man has this problem. You gotta disease? Cure it. It's your problem. And ya kin tell them somethin' else too. The next riot ain't gawna burn our homes down. They'll be yours too. Y'hear? Tell'em. Make'em listen, because, baby, this town's gawna burn."

"And Mickey? Did you settle his fate, Paul? Should he hide under the bed?"

"I said don't push me on it! I'll take care of him when the time comes!"

"You won't protect him?"

"No, no, no! Leave me alone!"

"Paul?"

"Goddamit, Tom, I said to shut up—and I mean it. I'm not talkin' about this. If you don't can it, I'm leavin', you hear? Got no time to fool around anymore!"

"O.K., Paul."

The entire group waited expectantly to see which of the two would come out on top. It was just one more crisis to be resolved in thirty hours of crisis since Thursday night, when their world had been shattered by the death of Martin Luther King. The parents and even the young militants—the violent ones who had rejected his nonviolence, the philosophy of Gandhi and Jesus—especially the young, were stunned and infuriated by the irrationality of the murder. Why hadn't they gotten Stokely? Why, Why? How could they express the fury that was eating their guts? How could they show that they were not apathetic, that they cared? Did they have to go out and burn to show they cared? Here was Paul, one of their school "M" senior leaders. Paul had all the qualities a leader needed. He was dynamic, bright, a good student, good-looking. He'd go to college—there was no question about that. He'd be a lawyer. If he lived long enough! If he made it through college. If he could control his burning fury today.

How he hated them, all of them, every white. No, not Mickey, not Mickey's parents, Dr. and Mrs. Cohen. They weren't white inside. They were black—felt black and understood black. They were soul friends—Jewish blue-eyed soul sisters and soul brothers. They were a part of him, not of the whites. They had proved themselves. They were real. It was always a battle in himself to separate his hate and his love.

He waited, tense and expectant, waiting for Tom to attack again. But his almost crouchlike expectancy wasn't necessary. Jim had picked up the gauntlet.

"Paul's right. Whites can't ever be trusted. It's their fault that Martin died—as much as if Dr. Middleman used the gun. Every goddam whitey has taught his child to think of us like sh--, step on us, to make servants of us and get rid of us when we make'em mad. I give up on'em!"

"So do I!" "Nothin'll ever change." Pessimism and cynicism coursed around the room.

"Nothin'll change because whitey won't let it change. They want us kept in our holes."

"Well, this is where it is. They didn't like Martin interfering with the low-paid garbage slaves. So they rubbed him out!"

Hopelessness, despair, were in the voice of each young person. They expressed a hopeless plea that the adults, Dr. Middleman and Tom, listen and do something—now, while there was still time. They wanted to be constrained from the dangers they were facing, for it would come. It was inevitable. A human couldn't continue living with this despair, with the self-depreciation, with the knowledge that his society didn't need him or want him, that he was undesirable flotsam.

But they couldn't let that society go scot-free for this malevolence. Their country would have to bear the punishment of the guilty. White society would have to be faced and impressed with the enormity of its crime for three hundred years; for the falseness of the Emancipation; for the today, 1968, with its facade of civil rights covering the slime of lies and greed and degradation of millions of blacks. Yes, the struggle had to come. It was too late for talk.

The parents had sat back this afternoon not taking part in the Open Talk Session as they had in the first of the seven meetings. They were here to discuss the normal concerns of normal adolescents. What was there they could say? Was this a normal time? Were these normal concerns? Heartbroken, they sat mute, listening to the hysteria of their children. They themselves felt the infusion of adrenalin disturbing their equilibrium. They could understand what was happening to the kids. How lucky for them that this talk session happened to have fallen at this time. Tom would know how to cool it. God knows they couldn't.

Martha Harkins sat sorrowing as she watched her Paulie and listened to him wrestling with his anger.

"Mrs. Harkins?"

"I want to listen first, Mr. Pierce."

"Mr. Scott, do you wanna say something?"

"I just wanna say a word. There ain't much to say. We been dished out a body blow. Nobody feels it more than me. But we gotta roll with the punches. We can't go off fightin' blind because some crazy white man killed Martin!"

"It ain't one crazy white man! See? Excuse me, Mr. Scott, but you're like all the old folks. Run scared all your life. Glad they let you be whatever y'are. They're all the same!"

"Yeh, they're all the same," Mrs. Johnson put in. "But what you gawna do? Ya gawna kill yourself or let them do it 'cause you're mad? They ain't gawna let you come but so near before they strike you down!"

"Not if we have good organization. That's the most important thing of all. An' that's what the black people were never allowed'a have. The whites on the plantations and the whites in so-called freedom won't let us get together. They're scared of us. But you wait'n see!" Jim ended his little speech with passion.

"What you want me to wait for? To see you on the ground bleedin'n dyin'? I see enough of that."

"But what do you want the young people to do, Mr. Graves?" Tom spoke. "Give'em some guidance. How do ya see the next few days? How can ya suggest they control their anger? They need to see that their parents feel the same in this tragedy. What can you say to them?"

"Mr. Pierce, I been on a dog's end of everything all a' my life. Nobody been poorer than me. I've been beaten, in prison on a false charge, an' been cold n'hungry. I've been through every misery there is. My son Reggie knows it. I tell my children all the stories 'cause I want'em to remember. They'll tell you; ain't much I forgot. My kids has the hurt in their bones 'cause I put it there for them to remember."

"And what are ya tellin' 'em now, Mr. Graves?"

"I'm saying don't let'em push ya to burn. Cool it like Mr. Pierce says. They wanna snare you. I say get your education. Don' let'em stop you from learnin'. I went to high school 'n I got a good job in the post office. I'm never gawna be a millionaire, but I ain't gawna be hungry. An' my children are gawna go to college. 'N that's what I'm saying. Let'em taunt you. Let'em call you nigger and you bite your lips 'n learn!"

"No! No, I won't let them do to me what they did to you. No

one'll ever call me nigger and get me to keep quiet! I'll murder'em first!"

"Paul, wait, cool it, man. Paul! don't go yet. Let's listen to Mr. Graves."

"I'm not interested, Tom. Excuse me, Mr. Graves, I don't mean to be fresh but it's a new ball game. No more doormat. We'll get our education. Don't worry about that! But we're gawna change this country. Yeah! We are! It's our country, only whitey doesn't know it. We'll teach'em! They killed Malcolm? They killed John Kennedy? They killed Medgar and Martin? They aim to kill any leader who can straighten out this lousy nigger-hatin' country. But we're not gawna lay down 'n let'em do it. They're not gawna make an old hag of my wife and force me to leave home so she kin get welfare. I'm not gawna rest easy until I teach whitey his lesson. That's what I'm gawna college for. To learn how to rub whitey's nose in it. And we will! Y'hear, Dr. Middleman, y'hear? Tell it to the white world—everyone of ya—scum of the earth! You'll never call me a lousy little nigger anymore! O.K. for now!"

This Open Talk Session was not a usual one or a normal one, and twice more in that week Tom Pierce met with the students and other "M" kids who heard they could "talk out their fear and anger."

This instrument, the Open Talk Groups, was available when it was needed, clearing a path for communication for intelligent and rational discussion and for a liaison with the parent world. Dr. Ruth Middleman and Thomas Pierce were the instruments for resolution. (For elaboration of this day's session, see Dr. Middleman's "On Being a Whitey in the Midst of a Racial Crisis," in *Children,* Vol. XVI, No. 3, May-June, 1969.)

> Every person wants to be convinced of his ability to achieve, but uses bravado, apathy, or aggression to protect himself against failure.

5

Building Self-esteem

If anyone had told Mervin Ross during elementary or junior high school that he ought to think of going to college, he would have laughed. He had all he could do to keep awake in his classes. He was always hungry. In fact, it was remarkable to him that he managed to get to school at all. Besides, he kept telling his mother that his getting a job would be more help to her and the seven children than listening to the teachers, who put him to sleep. Anyhow, he wasn't learning anything. He could read well, and he could do arithmetic. He ought to get a job. Then he could take the place of his father, who had died down south, somewhere.

Even with the welfare check, it was a struggle to make ends meet. His mother bought clothes at the rummage store, clothes Mervin hated to put on. As hard as his mother tried to keep them clean it was a battle, with eight kids and their mother sleeping in two rooms, eating and cooking in the kitchen. Despite the Flit and other poisons, roaches and flies lived comfortably with Mervin's family. The kitchen was also their living room. It was impossible to do lessons even if anybody wanted to. Mostly Mervin didn't bother with his lessons, doing just enough to squeeze through with a D or a C. His mom urged him to do better in school. And even though he would do anything in the world for her, he couldn't get interested in school.

What he would do was to lie on one of the three beds while the rest were in the kitchen fighting, playing, yelling. He liked the quiet of "his room" so he could read. This was his best recreation. When the other boys on the block got home from school they'd be back on the street in two minutes with a ball, a glove or bat—that is, if they didn't have a job after school.

Mervin undertook a tortuous hegira once each week, threading his way through the alleyways of West Philadelphia to the 40th Street public library. It took courage to make the trip because roving gangs came down from north of Market Street to take on loners. Nevertheless, Mervin made it into the building and waited for dark before emerging with four books clasped in his arms. This was treasure, more enjoyed than the wholesome food his body had always done without.

It was this voracious reading which gave him the good test scores while he was in junior high and this brought him into the Motivation Program in the tenth grade. His counselor and I were attracted to his gentle nature, his friendliness, the brightness of his eyes. His infrequent replies were terse, modest. He was thrown in with others who had ability and were being exposed to the same barrage of motivation energy. Slowly he caught on and was infected by the others. The classes became more interesting. The cultural trips made him a member of a group enjoying emotional experiences. By the twelfth year there was no doubt he would take one of the top scholarships with supplementary financial help.

We held an open discussion in the "M" '65 class, the first class to be graduated from the Motivation Program. Even this first class, with a mere two and a half years of concentration, had shown an unbelievable increase in the numbers of students accepted to college. The 1964 class, one year before the first "M" class, had seven college acceptances. The 1965 class had sixty-four as early as April in its senior year. It was in this open forum, something like a Quaker meeting, that Mervin said frankly he had never thought of himself as a college man until the first "M" meeting in the tenth grade. The astounding news that we considered him among all those smart kids capable of a college career was energizing. He who had never bothered to get more than a C in any subject began to pull down the A's easily in every subject. He loved what he was studying. This was more important to him than the college. He was enjoying school. For the first time he was out in front of the class. Today Mervin is in a doctoral program at Temple University. He'll be a clinical psychologist, which was probably foreshadowed by his self-analysis in the twelfth grade.

Martha Harkins had been a domestic for many years. She had three children and a husband whose life was spent at menial jobs. The thing she knew from the moment her first child was born was that she'd wash floors all her life so the child could be educated out of poverty. Her oldest child was in the Motivation Program at Thomas Edison High School, a handsome, bright football player. The one thing lacking in him was the ingredient missing in most unmotivated people: he didn't think much of himself. First, he had had too much mediocre academic achievement through his early grades. Secondly, he was very dark complexioned, which didn't help his image. But his prowess as a ballplayer was the first step in the development of his self-love. From then on everything he touched was positive. He wanted to experience everything, every cultural event, including the Motivation Summer School at the University of Pennsylvania, so he could study "The Ethnic Backgrounds of the American People." He had to be ready for Cornell. In the senior year he took a scholarship to that college for his academic work, although his football record could have given it to him, an all-American from every point of view.

I got to know him when his coordinator, Louise Winston, recommended him for the summer classes. But beyond the pleasure of knowing this fine young man was that of working with his remarkable mother. Hers is a story of human motivation.

Physically she was not a good-looking woman. She was very tall, a bit stout and rather ungainly. Her jaw was unusually large and thrust forward. But her eyes were intense in their dark interest, their darting curiosity, their intelligence and sympathy.

Building Self-Esteem

From the beginning of the Program at Thomas Edison High School in 1967, Mrs. Harkins became an active "M" Parent at the meetings and a chaperone for cultural events. The first moment she attended the opening meeting she joined the telephoning committee. A personality often declares itself by the kind of committee the individual joins. In this case, Martha wanted to be in touch, to communicate with others. This was her first effort to broaden her own scope. Soon she offered to undertake a role in the Open Talk Sessions that our psychologists conducted for seven consecutive weeks serving "M" students and parents. In the parent sessions I was impressed by the sensitive understanding she expressed in homespun English. The "black English" with which she set out her concepts of human needs and relationships between the two generations had more professional validity than the books used in the university courses. With all her ungainliness she had a physical and mental attractiveness to the adolescents. They "dug" her because she related to them. She was as much at home in the high school world of her teen-age son as she was in the eight-year-old world of her youngest child. They could relate to her further because she had not lost the burning indignation which is part of the black man's soul. She was a militant, like them, and in 1967 the militancy of the black student was just beginning. What was important for us and for them was that she meant to harness the militancy and indignation to help her people. Black was a new banner—not Negro, black!

About this time she became a nonteaching assistant at the school. This was the first step upward in the "rise of Martha Harkins." There were small incidents which composed the colorful mosaic of this new friend. When I had completed and published the humanities curriculum, her first reaction was to ask if I would approve of and lead a group of "M" Parents undertaking some of the units in a one-night-a-week class.

During the summer when her son came to the University of Pennsylvania to take the "Ethnic Backgrounds" humanities unit, the parents were encouraged to come to hear the ethnic lecturers. Martha came, took notes, asked questions. All the time she read, read, all the suggestions in the humanities, books on race relations, problems of our society.

One day she asked me shyly if there were such a thing as money to help older people get a high school diploma—some small sum so she could get some proper clothes, fares, and school needs. I shared the project with a black attorney in the city who had small funds for such deserving causes. Within one school year Martha completed the courses and received her diploma. More miraculous than this was the fact that Temple University offered her matriculation in evening courses with scholarship help. It was in this summer before beginning at Temple that she joined thirty Motivation seniors I was preparing for college entrance with an intensive course in composition. There was much reading, discussion of morality, philosophy, people. Her compositions at first were blustering efforts to express eloquent thoughts. By the end of the six-week summer school her essays had taken form. Over and over she wrote the paragraphs, polishing, changing. From the hot summer class she ran to a hot job to earn a living, for there were still two adolescents and a sick husband at home.

Martha calls me occasionally to try on an idea for size or to ask my help in some writing problem. These are simply intellectual exercises. She is a completely motivated, developed human being who understands her potential.

The thing I came to realize that first year of the Program, as "M" fathers and mothers met each third Thursday evening, was something I'd forgotten myself as my own children came through their adolescence. As adults we simply put our own puberty and all memories of it out of our lives when we become parents. The years between the parents' marriage and the child's entrance into adolescence becomes a hiatus—an unbridgeable chasm with the "imbeciles, parent-haters, destroyers of self and family, monsters" on one side and the all-wise, despotic, but loving parents on the other.

The parents, repositories of all wisdom and judgment, have

Building Self-Esteem

forgotten the turmoil and the anxieties of those years. They don't remember the embarrassment they felt exhibiting a face full of pimples, the frantic battle with the angry pustules; the self-doubts; the pains or discomforts of menstruation, irrational sexual heat; the emotional highs and lows; the daydreaming all day, or simply, colossal apathy.

Of all the growing-up phases, it's puberty that imposes the greatest stresses on both child and parents, and it's precisely at this time that most parents stop their own intellectual and biological memory. We succumb frequently to a throwback, fixing all morality and activities, even dress and hair styles, as most correct and decent only as it was done in the days of the parents' adolescence. And with each such recollection—"When I was your age!"—the parents reinforce their unhearing and obdurate ignorance. We mean to help and protect the child, but it cannot be done by shutting ourselves out of their lives. On the contrary, we must draw on the best of our experience to form the base for the best of the new generation's life by talking, participating, creating, changing.

I encouraged the "M" Parents Group to bring their problems to the monthly meeting where they could share the concerns with each other.

One of many productive discussions stands out in my memory.

David Ludwig, chairman of the "M" Parents Group, was conducting the session, inviting the parents to share any problems they might have and to direct them to me. For a few minutes he coaxed. Finally Mr. Castor raised his hand, timidly. His low voice could hardly be heard in the small auditorium.

"I'm worried about my son, Mrs. Segal. He's a good boy and he's proud to be in the Program. This is the first year I've seen him study this way. But his mother and I are worried." Mr. Castor went silent.

"Mr. Castor," I called, "what are you worried about? Is it something you'd like to share with other parents?"

"All right. You see, I'm a plain man. My wife does housework and I'm a baker. But we have respect for education and a good clean life." He stopped again and Mr. Ludwig urged him on.

"The trouble is, I don't know how to deal with this new thing. It's not like John at all. My wife was cleaning under his bed and found a book, a sex book. She was horrified and so am I. She put it back, but we don't know what to do." A murmur and some laughter had started among the parents. Mr. Castor sat down, embarrassed. A hand went up.

"I'm James White. I'm not laughing at you, Mr. Castor. I'm laughing because I thought I was the only one with that problem. When I found the stuff under Jinny's bed, I really let her have it. That's the last I ever saw of it." A woman raised her hand.

"I don't agree, Mr. White, with that way. If you made her feel like she's a criminal, she'll read it somewhere else." A fourth hand went up.

"I want to ask how many parents here are aware that their children sneak this stuff in to read?" Over fifty hands went up. I took the mike.

"Look around, parents." Their heads turned in all directions and they laughed aloud at the meaning of what they saw.

"You see, these parents whose hands are up know their children are reading those lurid books. The other half do not know their children are reading them. And indeed they are all experimenting with forbidden literature. What does it mean? How many women here read *True Romances* and *True Story* in your youth?" Every woman's hand went up. "How many men read the underground cartoons of Popeye and Tillie the Toiler?" Almost every hand rose.

"Isn't the answer obvious to all of us? We've all come through the same attractions in our adolescence. We read and hid the same stuff our youngsters are reading and hiding because they've been taught that sex is a taboo subject. But did the reading damage you? I'm sure it didn't. I would recommend you pay no attention, Mr. Castor. Depend on the training you've given your children to help them over this time." Another parent called over: "You're also breaking into his privacy if you tell him what you found. He has to feel he can keep something to himself." They had helped each other to a new understanding of a perennial problem. This was one of many niggling concerns that they were able to share with each other and me.

Sometimes they brought to my attention some class situation that needed correction. This was brought to the department head, the counselors, or when necessary, to the principal. Sometimes I heard wild stories brought home by the children. Miss Toth was drinking liquor in class right out of a milk bottle and did no teaching. Anyhow, the whole class got A's on their reports. This was pre-union by just three years. Delicate to handle? Miss Toth was transferred to a less demanding class. But she was retained in the school system when she should have been sent off for rehabilitation. There are too many such sick people foisted upon helpless children.

The "M" Parents were a warm, interesting group, and I looked forward to each monthly meeting. There were a few middle-income, white and black families, a few professional fathers and mothers, since we were part of the University complex, and we had "sold" the professors on our program. The remainder were low-income, quite poor, uneducated fathers and mothers or just mothers. Several months after the forming of the "M" Parents Group, Mrs. Bolen made a heartfelt statement on the floor.

"Mrs. Segal, I want you to know something. I work hard all day cleaning other people's houses. I come home tired at six o'clock, throw a dinner together, clean up, take a fast wash, get dressed and run over here to the meeting. I love to come, Mrs. Segal. It makes me feel good every time. Nothing short of sickness would keep me from coming." It was a thrill to me to listen to her and hear the applause, meaning that the rest of the parents agreed. The organization woman in me was pleased because I saw that the opportunity for interaction with the speakers, who came from every profession to address them and to be questioned by them, was a broadening experience, giving them an "ego lift." That Judge J. Sydney Hoffman, a friend and admirer of the Program and a most understanding friend of Philadelphia youth, came frequently to speak to and with them, and to be available for the "M" students, was a great compliment to them.

The fact that parents were asked to chaperone the "M" students on their bus trips to New York and Washington, or on their visit to the governor in Harrisburg, and that they were able to serve as chaperones when the students attended concerts, operas, and plays, being admitted at the same reduced fee, was considered a privilege.

It was they who had decided early in the game what kind of parents group they wanted. They wanted to participate, and they wanted to have the same cultural experiences the students were having. I was happy with their requests, for I hoped the parents would grow with the children and not be left on the other side of a cultural gap. If communication was to be established between them, they had to have similar experiences to discuss, to share pleasure in.

Every meeting's program was designed to focus, in some way, on their "M" students. The speaker might be a psychologist, a district attorney, a judge, an artist. The plan for the meeting was constructed so that it would eventually lead to the enrichment of the parent and students.

It was a unique organization in the inner school system of the '60s. In the past those schools with a large white, middle-class majority had an active parent-teacher group, which met frequently. Even so, they were merely tolerated by the administration, which permitted them only fund-raising activities for the purchase of supplies and equipment they could not get from a miserly, poorly operated school system. It was a rare parent who dared make demands. It was a rare parents group that dared inject itself into the workings of the school. That was the principal's territory, and he intimidated anyone who encroached.

As the ethnic character of the inner schools changed, the

parents, timid, cowed by memories of repressive teachers, and overwhelmed with tiredness after the long working day, took no part whatsoever in school activities. I remembered that when I was a child in an immigrant family in South Philadelphia, our parents—Jew, Italian, Pole, all immigrants—were cowed and repressed in the same way, disdained by the WASP administration and teacher. There were no parents groups. Most often in the '60s, too, there were no parents groups. After report cards, a sprinkling of mothers would show up to talk timidly to a teacher.

With the advent of the Motivation Program, a fairly sudden change had come about in West Philadelphia High School. At least forty-five parents of the initial 135 "M" students were attending a monthly meeting. As the second and third groups came in the following two years, giving us a body of 470 "M" students in a school population of 3,500, we rarely had fewer than a hundred parents attending the meetings. Mysteriously, many of the silent or nonexistent fathers appeared, too. On teacher-visitation days, the parents came dressed in their best to discuss their children's progress. The parents were exhibiting a new proprietary concern for their children's education.

Why I wasn't brought down to the front desk or to the central office and chastised for inciting those parents, I don't understand. For I was indeed doing that, although I didn't recognize it as incitement when I said to them in that first hour, the working hour, of the monthly meeting: "If you have complaints about the education your children are getting, what are you doing with those complaints? Why are you not bringing them to the school?" I didn't recognize it as incitement when I said, in answer to an aggrieved parent who had gone to the teacher and had felt beaten: "It's your school, not the teacher's or the principal's or the superintendent's. Your taxes pay for this school. If you're not satisfied with the answer you get from the teacher, go to the principal. If you're still dissatisfied, go to the district superintendent or to the very top. Why are you timid? They are your civil servants. This is your property."

It was this kind of promotion which began to motivate parents to request, then demand change.

I had learned early in my organizational career, when I worked devotedly for overseas children in ORT schools, that the greatest program in the world would die aborning unless it received fine planning and concentrated promotion. The program itself needed motivation—that is, stimulation from without. Here was an unbeatable program, the education of one's own children—at home, not 8,000 miles away, as in ORT. The cause was there, and I proceeded to apply my strong convictions to the goals of the program, acting on my belief that all parents want the best for their children; that, given integrity and direction, they will make the goals come about. This was the fabric of the "M" Parents Group of the Motivation Program.

> The desire for the respect and trust of peers and teachers was a prime motivator.

6
Crisis in Discipline

Being the Motivation coordinator was the same in the beginning as it is today in fifteen high schools of Philadelphia. This person undertakes to make the group of three to five hundred students in the school her immediate concern. She is concerned with everything about them, taking pleasure in their successes and feeling sadness in their problems.

It was and is the concern of the coordinator to promote and to uphold school law with her students, but I believe this person must essentially teach honesty and respect, repudiating specious, irrational behavior, no matter who is at fault.

We had built up a mutual respect between the first 470 students of the three "M" classes and the "M" staff. The students, now sophomores, juniors, and seniors, held discussions during the monthly "M" meetings about attitudes, responsibilities, and the behavior that is proper in various places. Then, as today, "M" students received compliments from bus drivers, theater and concert managers, from "hosts," for the mature behavior of our young people.

One hundred forty "M" '66 students were taking the annual trip to New York City one Friday during their senior year. There was a teacher and a parent on each bus. It was a tiring day, but one filled with experiences the students would remember—the stock exchange, Rockefeller Center, the United Nations, sharing the goodies from lunch bags, singing, enjoying the comradeship. At 10:00 P.M., on the way home, we stopped at a deserted Howard Johnson's on the New Jersey Turnpike. The students, who had not stopped eating for one minute since the bus had left Philadelphia at 7:00 A.M., now rushed into the restaurant, starved. Within a few moments Tom Campbell, a well-liked teacher and leader of bus number one, came to me to say that a father had overheard a conversation while he was in a men's-room cubicle. Students on bus number two were drinking wine.

I took the mike and laid the discovery before the class. Everyone seemed genuinely horrified. We discussed how this might endanger the Program as it applied to their future. Finally I threw the gauntlet down and said I wanted to find the bottle on my seat when I returned to the bus. The students left the restaurant while the adults waited. I returned to the vehicle. No bottle. In a moment Robert Dixon brought me the empty wine bottle, which he had found in the trash basket. Nobody talked or ratted. The trip to Philadelphia ended miserably for all. We all knew that the incident could not be taken lightly.

The next morning, Saturday, parents were calling me to find out what had happened. Their children had reported—not that they had partaken but that others had put wine in the Cokes in the back of the bus.

Monday morning I waited in the principal's office to make my report. Someone had already spilled the beans.

"Well." He regarded me sternly. "You see how impractical you are? This idealistic trust you have in the kids will get you into trouble someday. You see what happens when you don't impose strict discipline? What do you have to say about it? They'll have to be punished."

I agreed that the students had let me down, had violated my trust, but it was a very small group out of the whole class. I asked him what he had in mind as punishment. He would think it over, he said, but administratively he could not allow this misdemeanor to go unpunished. I asked him to give me a few days to find the guilty ones.

"How do you expect to find them?" He laughed at my blind trust. "Will they come to you and confess?"

"I think they will," I answered meekly. "Let me try."

"All right, I'll give you until Wednesday, and if you can get the guilty ones to own up, I'll relent and let them off fairly easily." I felt he was amused with me.

Where was I to begin? For two hours the "M" office had a funereal atmosphere. I knew our beautiful program was coming down around my feet.

Two of the seniors, Robert Dixon and Robert Jefferson, came in to talk to me. What was to happen? I discussed with them the principal's concession. Would they help me find the students who had participated in the drinking? They would try. For two days the entire "M" '66 class was in turmoil. Nothing was happening in class, no homework was done, the home phones were banging away. Back and forth both Bobs went, coming to me and returning to their peers to negotiate. I promised that I would help them with a fair punishment, but a punishment they would have to suffer. They could not expect the administration to overlook their actions. Back and forth the two emissaries went, and finally they returned with the news that there were eight guys who were ready to own up. But they wanted to do this at Thursday's meeting of the "M" group. They wanted no one there but me.

I opened the meeting and announced immediately that because of a very serious matter, I was turning over the discussion to Bob Dixon. When I had taken my seat, Bob recounted quickly what all knew. They'd been living with it since the previous Friday evening. My talk with the principal and the details of the negotiations were shared. Finally Bob asked the eight to stand. I was dumbfounded. Eight of the brightest young men in the class had used the bottle of wine. The decency of these young men, to want to admit to the misdeed openly, the willingness to face their peers! For three years we'd impressed on them our belief in their potential and their integrity. They were rising to the challenge.

Now it was my turn to negotiate with the principal. He couldn't believe the students had confessed, let alone publicly. He hadn't come to a decision. I could understand his deep concern, for as he said, an administrator had to think about the effect on the entire school. He hadn't decided on the punishment. He wanted to meet the parents. "When?" "Next Tuesday." I pleaded with him. It was already a week that the students had been suffering for their misdeed. We were asking them to go through a weekend, five days more. They weren't studying for exams; college boards were coming up. Why couldn't he decide on the punishment? Drs. Brancato and Washco, the two vice-principals, urged him to make a decision, but the principal wanted to discuss the matter with the parents. I felt his concern, but the delay was brutal; the days were unbearable for all, including the administration. Each evening, all evening, all weekend, "M" parents, those of the guilty eight and the many others who had become close in our "M" Parents Group, were calling me. All were disturbed about the misdeed itself, but they were indignant about the delay.

Tuesday morning the parents, the parents' chairman, the vice-principals, the principal and I met. The principal went over the matter and wound up with a dire statement concerning the punishment he was working out. He was about to leave. Mr. Vaughn spoke up, angry, at last expressing the outrage the parents felt at this inhuman treatment, these unreasonable delays. Other parents spoke up supporting Mr. Vaughn's torrent of words. They'd taken time off from work. What was the decision? What was the punishment? The principal was caught in his private dilemma. Being a good administrator dictated one course; being a sensitive human being suggested another. No answer. At last, I was called.

This was it. He told me he'd decided to put the eight on temporary exclusion from the Program for several months. This would be a lesson to everybody. He felt that with the rapid changes going on, liquor, drugs, it was best to make an example of the boys for the sake of the larger number of students in the school. Everyone would benefit from the example. He asked me to convey the punishment to the students. I realized how hard this was for him, but I felt sick. My awe of the principal left me. In my anger I told him how I felt about the punishment and the cockeyed injustice of the affair. These were fine boys, seniors. If they were to be put out of the program for a while now, their grades would go way down. It was almost time for the transcripts to go to the colleges. A boyish prank, one for which they'd already suffered a week and a half, would ruin their chances for college. And where would he expect them to hang out if we put them out of Motivation classes—on the fire escape?

I wouldn't convey the punishment. I had conveyed the bargain and it had been broken. My standing and effectiveness with the students and parents were gone. The Program could not flourish under my supervision any longer. I would apply for a transfer out of the school and he would have to get another coordinator. I left his office, heartbroken. Twenty students were crowded into the "M" office waiting to hear the verdict. They read it in my face and their moods matched mine. I was serious. I no longer wanted to stay here. How could the students believe me any longer? I'd betrayed them.

Soon Dr. Brancato came to convey an olive branch. I understood the action. An opening for peace had been made. I returned to the principal. What, he asked, would I consider a suitable punishment? My answer came quickly. No participation in any cultural experiences, sports, trips for three months. All other responsibilities had to be met. No mention of the escapade on the transcript. The principal accepted my recommendations.

I returned to my office, my joy scarcely concealed. No words were needed. Those students read me well. They were attuned to my moods. We had something going!

We emerged from this near-catastrophe with a stronger program. More important, the students and parents had a new sense of my determination to stand with them, behind them, wherever I was needed. But we'd started life together, "M" '66 and I, with a binding grief. Sadness brings people together.

Talk about the coincidence of personalities and events! This class, "M" '66, had a coincidence of great kids—high-spirited, needing reining, but bright, good, outgoing as a class, and sensitive to pain.

It was this same class that had lived through a trauma three years before on the day of its induction into the Program.

Friday, November 22, 1963, the class of tenth-graders with their fathers and mothers, all of us dressed to the teeth, came to Drexel University to participate in the students' induction into the Motivation Program. Dr. Allen H. Wetter, the superintendent of schools, was there with the "M" gold pins. Also present were Dr. Harnwell, Dr. Osol, and Dr. Bonnell of our three universities. A pall lay over the very still group, for enroute from West Philadelphia High School we'd learned the President had been shot in Dallas.

No ceremony was started. All waited as if frozen by the bizarreness of what was happening. At last the announcement was made: the President was gone, irretrievably, the young, handsome President with whom every youth had identified. The aborted ceremony was over. But the shared tragedy made me a guide and friend.

This is the role of the coordinator of the "M" Program in each of the fifteen schools. The "M" Group is an island in the school albeit not separated from the rest of the students. But the difference lies in the concentrated concern of the coordinator and her staff for the total welfare and enrichment of the "M" student. This condition continues to serve as an example to the school with three thousand students where everyone is a number, all are anonymous, alien. Life is fragmented. Yet the larger numbers take pride in the academic excellence that is emerging.

The quality of the program depends largely on the quality of the coordinator's dedication. In the five years since the program became part of the additional fourteen schools, four men who were excellent coordinators have moved upward into ad-

CRISIS IN DISCIPLINE

ministrative positions where they will be able to apply their Motivation Program philosophies to other groups of children.

In these few years, too, we have made several errors in the appointment of people who made glib, warm impressions on the sophisticated examining committee. They slipped by and we were constrained to appoint them. It is the students who alert us to our error. The young sniff out a fake very quickly. They knew when a coordinator is there for his own advancement, not theirs. Fortunately, the two serious errors have worked themselves out of the job by their own overzealous self-interest.

The quality of the "M" coordinator and staff makes an impression in many ways: how the "M" students have been trained to responsible leadership and citizenship in the school, how creative the cultural organizer is, how creative and motivated "M" teachers are, how the community resources are brought into active cooperation for the development of the students, how active "M" parents are. The coordinator must be a researcher, seeking out possible solutions for her students' problems; she must try to organize change. For instance, we found serious shortcomings in the way we were diagnosing and aiding children's needs and potential. This failure was due to the anarchic educational structure in which no articulation existed among the classes and grades of one school in any district and the classes and schools into which they fed from level to level. If the attitudes and performance of a given teacher were poor, mediocre, or spotty in any grade, this year became the hiatus in the child's school life from which he might or might not ever recover. It became a matter of luck. The third-grade teacher then taught the "slow kids who were dumped into her room according to their low level." For millions of people, this process has spelled the end of intellectual growth.

As I read the precipitous drops in IQ in the students' iron lungs from third grade upward, I decided I wanted to try a small experimental project in articulation. Dr. Carl L. Fromuth, superintendent of District One, my own district in those days, liked the idea and provided me with associates from the elementary and junior high schools that fed into West Philadelphia High School. I met with John D'Angelo, principal of Barry Elementary School, and Dr. Philip Davidoff, principal of Shaw Junior High School (and now a member of the Board of Education). We planned and pinpointed what could have had far-reaching effects. But a new administration came into the school district and more urgent priorities put our experiment to rest.

Just as in this instance we put our talent to rest, so we do with all of our national human resources. When a person's age reaches the magic number of 65 he must retire, ready or not, and thus much wealth is lost to us in our leadership. A short time ago Isadore Klingsberg, formerly math head at West Philadelphia High School and one of my associates, served as consultant for our annual Motivation humanities and math teachers' seminar. He came back from retirement to stimulate and motivate and to help them create new techniques to grab the kids. What a pity, I thought, as I watched him teach experienced teachers in the workshops, much as I used to sit in on his own classes at West High. What a pity to let this man retire, a man who can teach math as an art or the art of math. Either way, the day was an exciting experience. His directions for that day started a course of math articulation for "M" feeder schools which was taken up by the math leadership.

It's all in the quality leadership on top level, and Alex Tobin, director of mathematics education for the School District, is of such quality. We are undertaking an articulation project for mathematics, recognizing potential "M" students in the feeder junior high schools as early as seventh grade. These students will be rostered to a two-year Algebra I, in eighth and ninth grades, in which the students will develop not only an understanding of algebraic concepts but in which they will utilize learned and nonlearned fractions, percentages, etc. The students will then move into the high school "M" Program well prepared to take Algebra II, or Geometry, or what we hope will be a tenth–eleventh year unified, concurrent Algebra II and Geometry course. This we feel will provide us with math scholars and/or with students who will not be terrified by the thought of higher mathematics.

This articulation must be undertaken in all disciplines if we are ever to give children stimulating and logical intellectual development through their school lives. Unfortunately, I do not see or read of any such activity in English arts, social studies, foreign language, or vocational arts. Nor should the task be considered an impossible one. Given the organizational structure in Philadelphia and cities that use the same scheme, each district can undertake such articulation successfully.

And while the coordinator is promoting and guiding such activities as the above, she is responsible for creating a new breed in the large urban school/factory. This is a breed that is proud to engage in intellectual and cultural pursuits while it remains a contemporary being with its peer group. The coordinator must be the director of all these efforts.

The coordinators and the cultural organizers are a determined group. Peg Killian at Lincoln, Alice Boles at Roxborough, and Tobe Amsterdam at Olney fight a continual threat of reduced funds by seeking out the "freebies." Gayl Haaz at Kensington opens wide her torrid eyes when a roster man threatens the integrity of one "M" student's roster for the following year. It comes around to individualized caring.

Every type of special attention has its reward, and the coordinator must fit the reward to the deed. The kind of attention the "M" students and their activities receive from the communications world in the persons of Frank Ford and Jerry Stevens of the local radio, Len Lear of *The Philadelphia Tribune*, John Gillespie, Linda Citro, and Peter Binzen of *The Evening Bulletin*, gives the students and parents pride in their program. The approbation of the adult world is vital to the development of this pride. But the coordinator must take the lead in bringing understanding to the community.

It is a sad commentary that many people who lead generally untraumatized lives and should therefore develop objective judgment of conditions, of human problems, are nevertheless unwilling to see the problems in another part of the forest. These are the good people on the middle and upper income levels who thrive psychologically and economically on the subgroup—those who have the least mobility. This group is joined by a sprinkling from the low income level who must also have those in a position inferior to their own so that their own status might be served.

Thus, the very people whose education or experience should have prepared them to understand society's problems and possible cures are the very ones who should offer their understanding and support. Instead, they thrust blame on those unfortunates who can do the least to help themselves. The blame is fragmented, often irrational. The carpers rail against the welfare system, cloaking their hardness with puritanical judgments against a woman's illegitimate children or the spending of money on frills such as a second pair of shoes or a television set.

Or, the blame lies with permissive judges for letting offenders off too easily; with parole boards for letting sex offenders, murderers, and thieves out to prowl again before they've paid their debt to society (—not until rehabilitated, but until they've paid their debt to society!).

Or, "they're lazy," and that's why "they're poor." Or, "the police are soft on them."

"They" are some other part of society, and each ailing entity is responsible for its own illness and its own cure.

The most flagrantly derelict and inept organism, the critics say, is the school community in all urban centers of the country. The schools are considered repositories for the total child, all children, and are charged with the responsibility for erasing all that happened to a child in his first six years, and for the infusion in the following twelve of a thirst for knowledge, the motivation to achieve, and aspiration toward lofty goals. The same critics look quickly at retarded reading levels, at dropout rates, at turmoil in schools, at poorly prepared graduates, and they flagellate the school for failure to provide education to the youth of their city. Nor do the critics make a cause-and-effect association. Society's malaise has no relationship to the students, as the critics see it.

Without any doubt, the schools—that is, boards, administrations, teachers—have indeed failed in their charge. But it is not the school alone that must bear the sole responsibility for either the child's education or the system's failure. As critical as I am of schools and their practices, it is nevertheless completely unjust and simplistic to use them as the whipping boys for the rest of us.

For it is the rest of us who are responsible—for our unmelted ethnic hatreds, for the creation of the evils of poverty, the ghetto, ill health, crime, apathy. Each island of despair in our society is really a reflection of the problems of our larger community. We are not divisible; we are one in health and in travail. The ugliness and cynicism portrayed in the greediness of great corporations affect the life of the smallest, poorest child. The criminality in a great city makes it dangerous for a rich suburbanite to walk along either his suburban lanes or the asphalt of the city. We are interdependent, our lives are interwoven, whether we want it or not. Thus, the recalcitrant third-grader is giving us a signal, loud and clear, of what he will mean to us as an adolescent or adult. It is for us to listen.

It is the quality of our regard for our fellow citizen that forms the character of our people. We are a people who demean the brain of a black child, the personality of a Jew. The meanness of the dole, the lack of liberality in daily living, the punitive quality of our penal system, are in small measure our society's judgment of the worth of our fellowmen.

The same judgment is apparent in the public's apathy and disinterest in its schools that produced the chaos and the failure of the school systems. The citizens fail to consider the schools as their property, the neighbor's children as their children, their future work force, their future leadership. Antiintellectualism is our way of life. The citizens abdicated their responsibility as members of a democratic society. The school, a microcosm of our society itself, with all its negative characteristics, becomes a computer, where the input is error laden and the programmed end product a failure.

West Philadelphia High School was and is such a microcosm; a piece of the society around it, with all the same social failures that infected the life feeding the school. In 1963, West Philadelphia High School was about 90 percent black and a reflection of the ethnic community around it with all the ills and disaffections of a multifaceted society.

The most difficult part of establishing the Motivation Program in the early years was its promotion to the communities of University City and West Philadelphia; to the black parents and businessmen; to the white residents and businesses; to the teachers of the school, who were a bit of society; to the universities and the whites whom they wanted to attract back to the university area. This last had been a motivating goal for the colleges, to make the neighborhood safe and to provide good schooling for their professionals' children. Their interest in our experiment was not entirely a charitable effort. Indeed there was much of self-interest. But to their credit, the leadership of the University of Pennsylvania, Drexel University and the Philadelphia College of Pharmacy and Science was forward-looking. They saw the direction in which they would have to move in urban education during the '60s and they provided me with many facilities.

But the commitments to the Program of Dr. Gaylord Harnwell of the University of Pennsylvania and Dr. Allen Bonnell of Drexel had difficulty filtering down to some deans, some professors, some college students. A violent cathartic was needed to uproot the racism, the hatred and deprecation of others.

One lovely Friday afternoon, 160 eleventh-year Motivation students had bused the ten blocks from West Philadelphia High down to the University of Pennsylvania. I had set up an afternoon class every week for eight weeks. Each week the students had a different lecture and discussion with some of the University's most exciting cooperating professors. My students were eager visitors to "their campus," for had they not spent three days of their tenth year in the initial university visit? They'd begun to feel like potential college students. They had begun to project for themselves an image of a co-ed or campus man. Furthermore, they understood the lectures.

Occasionally a student asked to be excused. Marguerite W. asked to be excused that Friday because of her evening date, and being denied, attended with bad grace. Despite this, on Saturday afternoon Marguerite called me at home after the College Board exams to tell me excitedly how lucky it had been for her that I'd made her go to the biochemistry class at Penn the day before. "Because," she shouted happily, "the question about the composition of blood in the morning exam was exactly what we had yesterday!" The accumulation of knowledge was beginning to show.

On one Friday I arrived at 37th and Locust with the first of the three buses and led the students into the building. As the second and third busloads of my students came up into the building I was sensitive to a mood different from the enthusiasm of other Fridays. It was a fleeting thing. The classes started and I moved from room to room to observe and listen. But there was something different. On Sunday I learned what the problem was. I had set up an association with the "M" Parents Group so that any parent with a problem could call or see me any time, day or night, week or weekend.

Mr. Dodson told me of an unhappy incident that had occurred. As the students left the buses they heard raucous laughter and jeering coming from fraternity men who were hanging out of each window of one of the most prestigious old houses on campus. These were the frats which had never pledged a Jew or a Negro. They'd just invited in their first Pole. Ironically, this first Polish-American frat brother died in a frat-house fire at a Christmas party as a result of a boyish prank with "our Polack." But the incident involving our students happened long before they had felt that tragedy. From each mouth came the expletives that were painful to the pupils. "Look at the niggers in their Sunday-go-to-meetin' clothes!" "Look at the chimps wearin' clothes!" and with this the fellows on the porch jumped up and down and scratched themselves. "What ya doin' on our campus, Niggers? G'wan back to West Philadelphia with your peanut brains!" The presence of the white classmates seemed to infuriate the fratmen further. They, too, took some jeering.

I discussed the incident with the vice-president of the University, the following day. What could be done? The University did what it had to. But the harm to our students had been done. Those young men were a cross-section of our larger society and our attitudes toward each other. And the coordinator must be alert constantly to help the "M" students handle the problems.

Then there was the sophisticated young editor of the *Daily Pennsylvanian* who gave a blistering scolding to West Philadelphia High School for its cruelty in leading these poor Negro children on—making them believe they were capable of being Penn students. Her heart bled for these misguided children; there were painful philosophical qualifications that this young woman's biases had cooked up. From the lofty height of her senior-year experience *she knew the limitations of these poor kids from West Philadelphia High. We were perpetrating a hoax to promise what we knew was impossible.*

How does one explain away these painful and destructive blows to several hundred high school boys and girls who have never had any self-appreciation to begin with, who knew when they were little that they could never measure up to the whites, or to an older sister or brother. There was always someone or something to make the task impossible, someone to tell them that, no matter what, they could fail mainly because they were black or a minority or poor. How does one compensate for the feelings of unworthiness when these students read in a campus newspaper the headline *"Disadvantaged Students* to Visit PSU Campus Today"?

CRISIS IN DISCIPLINE

How can people lead productive lives when they are lacking a healthy self-love and are constantly reminded of their inferiority?

I had the privilege of seeing deeply into the souls of these young people. During one of the summer Motivation institutes, in response to the question, "Who Am I?" David wrote: "The first thing that pops into my mind is that I am David Adams, I am a nigger! I am a person who hopes to achieve greatness in a lifetime but I may not be able to do this because . . . I am a nigger! I am a person who likes to talk, read, and think. I am a member of the lower class in the United States. I am a person who is hated because he is Black. As you may have guessed I am a person who thinks a lot about race. I am a person who admires Adam Clayton Powell, Cecil Moore, Martin Luther King and others. Who am I? I am David, a thinker, a reader . . . a nigger! Who would I like to be? I would like to be one of the important Negroes of the day . . . Adam Clayton Powell, Cecil Moore, Senator Brooke. All of these men have money, Powell and Moore both have a mass of people behind them. (Powell has Harlem, Moore has the Negro gangs and adults concentrated in South Philadelphia but spread throughout the city.) Powell and Brooke both have seats in Congress and Brooke has the favor of the white power structure so long as he remains quiet in Congress. Moore has something else I want, he has a degree in law that says he is independent and doesn't need anything from anybody. I'm not sure which one I'd like to be, Powell, Brooke, or Moore."

Such choices one must face! But then, every man must have his heroes.

> Each student must feel that he is cared for by his home and his school community. He must believe that he is needed by his society.

7
Rescuing the "Throwaway Child"

The Motivation Program had all the components of the society around it. Not all the students selected initially and year after year were on the poverty level, although most were low income. Not all the parents became an active part of the program, although most of them indicated their deep desire to have the best for the children. Not all the students came from distressed, broken, or single-parent homes, although a large enough group of such "M" students made it more than an occasional misfortune. The saddest group were the children who had been cast off by their parents—"Throwaway Children," as Lisa Richette calls them in her poignant book of the same name. Judge Richette was deeply touched by Mark Quincey's story and related it there.

Mark Quincey was born in Korea about 1950 of a black American GI and a Japanese mother. The soldier considered the fornication a soldierly idyll and promptly forgot about it. Madama Butterfly had nine months to consider her problem, and finally, to get rid of her shame, she gave the newborn away. Actually, she never saw the child. This was the nameless child's first experience with rejection.

At three, the charming little toddler attracted the attention of a black NCO who was visiting the Korean orphanage. Besides wanting a child that his wife back in the States couldn't have, John Quincey was really taken with the beautiful, affectionate child. As soon as the truce was signed, Peg flew over and they adopted the boy and a girl from the orphanage. Mark came to the United States with his parents, and for the next nine years the four moved to one army base after another.

They settled in a New York suburb. It was an eventful growing up for Mark. But then, many a high-spirited, talented child can be a handful. Mark was just that—bright, artistic, eager, and needing a lot of love. Love he got from his father. It was his mother who withheld affection from the child. A confirmed alcoholic, she was increasingly neurotic about her sterility, and Mark and his sister had become the daily reminder of her failure as a woman.

When he was thirteen his father was killed in a car accident, and Mark, Jean, and her mother were left to continue their troubled association. The loss of John, her drinking, and the many problems all converged, and she took out her troubles on the children, beating them often and severely for every infraction of her rules. As a result, Mark took to staying away from home. His mother's tantrums were unmanageable and Mark came away from the beatings bruised in body and spirit.

I met Mark when he was enrolled as a tenth-grader in West Philadelphia High School, where he had been brought by his mother's aunt, a bitter old woman. As coordinator of the Motivation Program, whose goal was to seek out and develop students with a potential for higher education, I screened all entering students for inclusion in the special group. I was called into the organization room to talk to Mark when he registered. We knew only that his mother lived in New York, that his father had been killed, and that Mark and his sister had mixed ancestry. Nothing more. But everyone took to Mark. Although he cowered for a while, as a puppy will do when it has been beaten, he began to open up as he made friends among the students and teachers. Whereas his school record from New York was rather poor, his happiness now began to show in his improved class work and regular attendance.

The cultural activities were his greatest joy, and I knew that within five minutes of our opening the "M" office door, Mark would be there with his handsome Amerasian face and the joyous, deep voice.

"Hi, Mrs. Segal! What's new? What tickets did you get?"

And that week would be like every other. He did his homework, he went to a theater or a concert each week. He would take advantage of the Host Visit, another of the Program's activities devised to provide our "M" students opportunities for social experiences by spending an entire evening in the homes of many Philadelphia citizens. For him this was probably the most productive of the many projects, for his natural, outgoing personality bloomed in the free, rich atmosphere of the host's home. Mark sang for the eight or ten fellow students and hosts, there was heated discussion of random topics—the President's assassination the year before, the Freedom March, civil rights. Every topic was grist for the mill as the young "M" students felt the respect of the hosts for their youthful opinions. And lots of Coke and potato chips were consumed. Frequently as we left the homes, the hosts whispered their thanks to me that I'd allowed them to see the young generation in forms other than the stereotypes that were distasteful and threatening to them.

Mark finished his first year at West High. I was seeing him less frequently in his junior year, but I knew he was working in a grocery store from 6 to 10 P.M., five nights a week, in order to make money. He kept his weekends for studying and play of all kinds, and his gentleness and even temperament seemed unchanged.

I was shocked, therefore, to be called on the school phone by the juvenile detention center with the request that I come immediately concerning Mark Quincey. It was the last day of the school year.

He was one of many seated on a long wooden wall bench. He had on only an undershirt and jeans, both of which were badly soiled and bloodied. Ashamed, he came toward me and led me into an office where the examiner was waiting for us. The story horrified me.

The aunt in Philadelphia to whom his mother had sent him was no aunt. She was a casual friend who was willing to keep the boy as long as the mother was sending a portion of the father's pension check. But as her passion for alcohol consumed more and more of the check, the "aunt" gradually lost her pleasure in Mark. She wanted money for his keep. It was then that he got the grocery store job. Even so, everything he did bothered her—the way he looked, his room, his going to the cultural events, being an uppity nigger.

And then she wanted him out. His mother refused to have him back and the aunt lent him to her girl friend. It was at this point that Mark, seemingly so balanced, began to cry silently.

"Mark . . ." I touched his hand. "Why didn't you tell me any of this? We saw so much of each other. You could have shared it with me." I had made a mistake. My friendliness and concern had broken him down, and Mark made for the door. An officer appeared and offered to take him to the men's room. For one brief moment I caught his handsome coffee-colored face, pale and wet with tears, the Oriental eyes swimming, bright and sad.

Feeling a fast hatred of man and his cruelty to children, I turned back to hear the rest of the story.

"Mrs. Segal, I'm glad he left for a moment. It's a heartbreaking story but before he comes back, tell me how you see him."

"See him! Why did I come? He's a very fine young man, Mr. Johnson."

"Has he ever been in any trouble at school?"

"You're wide of the mark, sir. The boy is a favorite of teachers and students and he's never been anything but a joy to have around."

The door had opened and Mark took his place at the table.

"*At least* . . ." I gritted my teeth in anger. "At least they could have gotten him some clean clothes."

The examiner continued reading the record before him.

Mark was living with the aunt's girl friend and her lover while he went to school and worked in the grocery store. He was cleaning the house and even putting the dinner on for her so it would be ready for her and her boyfriend. And that's where the trouble came in. The boyfriend was a drunk, jealous and violent, and the evening beating of his girl friend became a ritual. Generally, Mark had already gone to his job by the time they came home. On the rare occasions they met, Mark tolerated the abuse directed toward him and escaped quickly.

Last night, many weeks after coming to live there, he had returned at 10:00 P.M. to find the drunken lover beating his girl friend. Mark grabbed the man's arms to restrain him, but this infuriated the drunk and, as if he'd been awaiting this opportunity, he threw himself on Mark, using superior strength to beat and bruise the frightened boy. Finally he grabbed Mark by his shirt and threw him out the door, warning him not to come back.

Again Mark realized he was not wanted and suddenly a secret yet unformed impulse sent him into the drugstore at the corner, where he usually went for an ice-cream cone and a friendly chat with Doc.

At this point Mark interrupted the examiner's narrative.

"Do you have to read the rest? I'll tell Mrs. Segal myself."

"I'm sorry, Mark, the law says I must read the entire thing as you related it." Mark hung his head and turned away from me. I realized there was something coming he didn't want me to hear. The story continued.

Telling the druggist that the girl friend had sent him for some kind of sleeping pills and razors, he took his purchase and began to walk.

For miles and hours he walked through West Philadelphia, and north into the lush green of Fairmount Park. There nestled among the ancient trees he found, to his amazement, a Japanese villa surrounded by an elegant garden and pond.

Some time later, a bicyclist passing the Japanese villa saw a human form under the light by the house and called police. Mark had taken several sleeping pills and had cut his wrists with the razor. He was brought to the hospital quickly and revived. This morning he was brought to the juvenile detention center, where he asked for me.

I was stunned and tearful at the same moment looking at this fine young man beside me. What must a human being suffer, to be brought to the point of self-destruction? How blind I was not to have felt his unhappiness. Why had he bypassed me and his counselor, who also had an attachment to him? Obviously we had failed him.

"Mark, why? What made you do it? Mark?"

Even in the quiet answer from a bowed head, one could feel the sensitivity, the artistic nature of Mark Quincey.

It was a fine evening, he said—warm, fragrant with the odor of trees and rotting roses in the tiny plots of the black neighborhoods. He walked through the crowded streets, which teemed with playing children escaping the heat of their boxy houses. Half-dressed adults sat on their marble steps chatting, friendly, relieved by the whisper of coolness. He felt lonelier than ever in the heart of this joviality. Where was he to go? Where would he be welcome? He walked for hours.

When Mark spotted the little tea house and recognized the Japanese architecture he felt an odd sensation; some distant memory had been summoned, although he could not grasp the image. What he decided firmly was that he would finish living here. He did not want to go on moving from home to home, not being wanted in any one of them.

He thanked me for everything I'd done for him and I cringed. I'd neglected him. I hadn't seen his pain these last few weeks, and he was thanking me!

Through some managing we arranged to schedule Mark's hearing before the judge within a few days. The mother had been brought from New York and had needed a few drinks to fortify her before her appearance. Her condition, her responses, the mute testimony on Mark's body to the old beatings, convinced the judge that hers was not a fit home for Mark.

We stood before the bar that morning, Mark in the middle, flanked on one side by me and on the other by one of our West

Philadelphia High School teachers who wanted Mark to live in her house. The judge questioned me about the boy. I told him how well liked Mark was by students and teachers: witness that one wanted him to live in her house. I told him that the boy was bright and talented. Did I feel, the judge asked, that Mark would go to college, even though his being in the Motivation Program implied that? There was no doubt, I answered, that with a stable home and support, he would be a scholarship student.

Mark was released in our custody, and I was to oversee his progress and report to the judge periodically.

The Motivation Program with its 450 students became his family for the next two years. This incident was the "moment of motivation" for Mark. Immediately upon graduation from high school he received an art award for a summer in Italy. That fall, he started with his scholarship at college. He will complete the last half year of college at Temple University. His painting is flourishing. He will make a good life for himself.

My belief in the individual and his vitality is renourished each day. In July, 1971, I met Clare Garner of that first "M" class coming toward me with one child in hand and eight ninths of a second child in the making. She had a B.S., and M.S., and a year in the classroom. Now she told me she would be going back to the University of Pennsylvania for a doctorate in administration. I am convinced that there can be many Marks, many Clares—the success stories that started very slowly, dully, badly, apathetically, and then went like a fireball in the twelfth year. Clare and Mark weren't exceptions. They were the majority.

That was still early in the game. We needed the understanding and help of everyone if we were to prove our point. The colleges were a vital partner in the plan and, at times, the humans who composed the universities were very trying. There were those professors and college students who viewed our program as a joke.

Early in the Program, during the years 1963, 1964, 1965,

the invasion by 160 black adolescents of the ancient academic halls or around campus was an occasion for neck-craning and wonderment. The concentrated effort around the country to recruit blacks didn't begin until later. Therefore, the first three classes of "M" students moving around the campus or sitting in on college classes made a profound impression on the white students and professors. Too frequently, their attitude was conveyed to the sensitive "M" students. In some instances, professors or instructors had not been involved in the planning of the three-day campus experience. These slips occur in any large organizational plan. Occasionally, teachers showed their annoyance, causing the young visitors to squirm with embarrassment. I learned with each experience not to take anything for granted. Every segment of the plans had to be tested. That was part of my multifaceted job as coordinator.

Despite the few uncooperative community and university people, the "M" students enjoyed the exposure each year. We were softening them up to the setting we said they might one day live in. They began to believe the promises made by the presidents of our three neighboring universities would come true. If they, the students, would produce, would prepare themselves academically, they would be admitted with as much financial scholarship aid as they would need. The promises were honest.

What we found in practice, however, was that the larger the college the more likely it was for the promises not to have reached all levels. Even when they had, deans did not feel bound by the commitments of the college president. Often the admissions departments made their criteria for admission more stringent than usual to "protect the underprivileged students." Admissions departments have their obscure standards for admission—so many children of alumni, so many from Philadelphia, so many from other states, so many Jews, etc. So many Negroes was not much of a problem in those days; very few applied. But it was the administration below the top who torpedoed the front-desk policies. Each dean or professor whose interest had not been sufficiently engaged, who brought his own hardened bias and preconception, helped us move two steps back when the one forward had been taken with such difficulty. Many of these, on the other hand, were willing to be on committees to help the underprivileged, not in concrete, long-range programs at the universities but in pathetic charitable projects in the ghetto communities. They set up organizations of their students to be part of our tutoring project. This short-term, remedial aspect of our program was provided by the visitors, community neighbors, and teachers of the school.

At this time too, the Philadelphia Tutorial Group came to offer its services. This was a group of Yale students who wanted to be of service to West Philadelphia's underprivileged children. Their impulse was commendable. However, I recognized fairly soon that, whatever their motivation or purpose in coming, they were not tutoring our students in geometry, French or physics. They were tutoring our students in ghetto problems, response to authority, and confrontation. That was the end of that source of community help. I've always wondered why they had to come to Philadelphia when New Haven has its own share of the underprivileged and unmotivated.

I've touched briefly on what was not done by our university partners in the program. It is what they did that added to the effectiveness of our work and to the exciting results. Each project was small, a miniature effort, but the payoff was tremendous. Individual professors made themselves available for weekly classes. These included people like Professor Samuel Noah Kramer, the noted Sumerologist; Dr. Robert Netting, anthropologist; Dr. Harold Levin, professor of social work; Professor Jerre Mangione, English literature; Dr. Tristram Coffin, professor of American civilization; and Dr. Edward B. Shils, professor of industry. All were authorities in their fields. All shared their time with us each week, broadening the students' intellects, motivating them to read in their subjects, enlarging self-concepts.

There was the "don" project, based on the image of the

Oxford University don. For example, three students met with Dr. Wallace Davies, professor of American history, in his home once a week for eight consecutive weeks, talking, discussing, reading about American history. Medical "dons," students at the University of Pennsylvania Medical School, became dons to individual eleventh- and twelfth-year "M" students. For eight weeks the "M" students accompanied their medical dons on some of their rounds, to lectures, to the labs, to watch rehabilitation. Twenty-five "M" students signed up for this project. Another ten wanted law "dons." Some wanted architecture dons. Today, with fifteen high schools in the Program, many of the colleges and professional schools provide these projects for their nearest "M" school. The purpose of the "don" project was not so much career orientation as giving the "M" students exposure to community problems and their responsive services.

Again, we tapped the community for its commitment. The Host Visit became a cornerstone project. I believed that there was more learning to be had outside the school walls than inside and that one of the richest sources was the homes of fellow Philadelphians. Of the four "M" seniors who visited Judge A. Leon Higginbotham, Jr., in his chambers, three are now in law school, inspired by his pride in black peoplehood, seeing that they, too, might make it. "Don't worry about getting into Ivy League colleges," he said. "Go to any college that will take you and learn as much as you can. Then get into the best graduate school for your specialty. Just keep going." Judge and Mrs. J. Sydney Hoffman, with their keen interest in adolescents and in the "M" Program specifically, invited fourteen to eighteen students to their home frequently for "Host Visits." Elegant Goldie Hoffman had a way of making others feel elegant and at home. The purpose of the visit was to create a social situation, communication between the two generations. This wasn't to be a career guidance evening. Only incidentally did the discussion rest on the host's profession. The evening was to have the quality of a party of friends and equals. The conversation may have started with a question about the host's career, but soon it moved to the all-absorbing concern: the Vietnam War. In 1965 the Host Visits were already preoccupied with the war, its wrongness, its immorality. The "M" students perceived the futility and wrongness of the war more often than the adult hosts. In 1971, the hundreds of "M" guests are still haranguing the older hosts about their responsibility to end the war. And then the talk went to drugs, vice, civil rights, and finally, some refreshment. It was a hopping evening with good talk and argument and anger. But always there were two excellent results. The young people felt their brains had been stretched. They came to school next morning pleased with the Host Visit, with themselves and what they'd learned. Above all they had been listened to by men and women of standing. They'd been listened to, argued with, and had sensed respect from the "old people."

The "hosts," on the other hand, were always grateful that they'd met a group of adolescents who did not fit the stereotypes of the burners and gang members. One host, an Indian who was a professor of Eastern religions, thanked us for having shown him and his family a different face of America. Judge Hoffman, with his keen concern for the problems of the youths he met daily in juvenile court, was especially pleased with the goals and the students of the "M" Program. To stimulate them, to help them experience democracy and the problems of their peer group, the judge initiated the Juvenile Jury. Twelve "M" students sat in the jury box of juvenile court watching the endless procession of society's young castoffs, listening to the evidence, to the pleas of heartbroken parents, to the frightened young offenders. And before the decision the judge instructed the "M" jury and asked for its verdict. Most frequently Judge Hoffman, and later, Judges Spaulding and Green, found the "M" jury's judgment more punitive than was warranted and the official decision then softened the verdict.

While this was happening, fifty other "M" students sat as observers in the courtroom. Their opinions of themselves had to be raised as they saw the respect accorded their peer friends in the jury box. Nor did Judge Hoffman stop with the jury. He drew all the "M" students into the juridical concerns of that morning, and the effects of the experience continued into the school activities in the days that followed. The "M" jury gave panel reports in the assembly at West High School. The importance of the project was that our young people, who, we felt, were to be the future leadership of our community, should be sensitive to the traumas as well as the pleasures of man around them. They had to know the stuff of which our society is made.

The human quality of the program inspired others to ask us for participation. One of these was an exceptional man, Anthony Amsterdam, Esq., a law professor at the University of Pennsylvania Law School. In 1967 he, his very bright, dedicated senior student Robert Ozer, and I devised a project called the Motivation High School Law Project. Third-year law men accepted an assignment to a Motivation high school where they would teach, in eight weekly installments, a course on "The Law and Society: The Responsibility of the Law to the Student and the Student to the Law." The course covered the most cogent aspects of the law as they related to the life of the student and his family. There were case histories, role-playing, and, at the end of the year, a seminar prepared at the University of Pennsylvania Law School for any of the students who cared to come. Three stellar figures in Philadelphia jurisprudence addressed these young men and women: Professor A. Leo Levin, Professor Anthony Amsterdam, and Judge J. Sydney Hoffman, our good friend. In the last few years, three area law schools participated in this productive program, the University of Pennsylvania, Temple University and Villanova University Law Schools combining the visits to courts with the school course. Noting the success of the Law Project in the Philadelphia schools, Columbia University initiated such a program in the New York public schools at that time. Dean Jefferson B. Fordham, after observation of a law class at South Philadelphia High School in 1967, indicated his intention to help promote similar projects in other law schools through a committee of the American Bar Association. Because the student's life with the community is considered essential by the Program, we are constantly seeking new associations and new projects for the "M" students. St. Joseph's College has provided us for the last four years with an advanced college-credit chemistry course, which is open to forty-eight "M" seniors and is directed by Dr. George Beichl, chairman of the chemistry department. Dr. Beichl's enthusiasm for the students and his continued romance with his own discipline enhance the prestige of the thirty-two-week Saturday course to the point where we have difficulty restricting enrollment to the forty-eight lab table spaces available. St. Joseph's College, Villanova University, Philadelphia College of Textiles and Science, Drexel University, and the University of Pennsylvania provide our "M" seniors with college-credit "college co-op" courses. The funding for these as well as our summer projects is contributed through the largesse of The Philadelphia Foundation under the direction of a warm individual, Sidney Repplier.

Philadelphia College of Pharmacy and Science and Temple University make their facilities available to us at all times. And all these colleges have been generous in scholarship help for our few thousand "M" students.

Philip Klein, pleased with the intent and quality of the Program, and devoted to his city's artistic affairs, has made available personal and foundation funds for our many educational and cultural needs.

It was the quality of the community's interest, its willingness to extend itself into the school and to embrace the students on the outside that convinced "M" students and parents that society cared for them. This knowledge was a great motivator.

Why did the Program work?

Right from the beginning, what were we doing that gave the projects vitality? There was so much happening in those early days that we didn't have the time to analyze, to keep controls or figures. We were planning the development of the

Rescuing the "Throwaway Child" 113

Program feverishly while we were getting the kids into the works, involving the boys and girls, the teachers, parents, community, and colleges. Everything was moving at one time. There was an excitement in the school, at least among the first tenth-graders we'd started with. Many of the teachers felt it and reached to the movement, some positively, some sullenly, with bad grace. But it was movement. We were shaking the apathy that had beset West Philadelphia High School.

We learned in that first year some of what motivated the Program and the children. It wasn't the extra equipment or machines we purchased that made the difference. It wasn't the superficialities that turned a diffident, self-deprecating adolescent into a more secure one, into one who began to trust in his future. It was the human relationships, the warmth and concern he felt from those around him that gave the student self-confidence and a new spirit of wanting to achieve. The crux of it all was to be found in the compactness of the group, the goals, and above all the personnel who were integrally attached to the students zeroing in on what had to be done. This was it.

The coordinator and her staff were the hub of the wheel. If that central person, the coordinator, was convinced of the correctness of the Program's philosophy and its goal, the first step was taken. If besides this, the coordinator, given status, was a strong personality who could "sell the product," that is, gain acceptance for the philosophy of the Program, the chances for success were great. If the coordinator, the cultural organizer, and the secretary believed in the potential of our young clients, if they could create the climate in which the students could believe in themselves, we could begin to make change. It was an investment we were making in the lives of the kids, and the goal was to cash in a few years from then.

I had hoped in those early years to provide the Program with its own site, outside the high school itself. The University of Pennsylvania was willing to share fourteen or fifteen rooms to house the Program on campus. This was one of the aims, to expose the kids, early, to the feeling of campus and of college worthiness—a goal served each summer in the summer "M" courses on the college campuses. But this idea died aborning, ten years ahead of its time. It wasn't until the fall of 1971, when Bartram High School's overpopulation had created difficult conditions, that my plea for the "M" Program on its own site fell on willing ears. This will be discussed in another context. Back in 1963, however, as we strived to prepare a climate in which we could do a convincing job with the students, our own personality traits were our major resource. Mrs. Fel, the cultural events organizer, Mrs. Aislee Hayes, our secretary, and I each brought a commitment and a love of children to our small enclave physically set in the heart of anti-intellectual West Philadelphia High School.

This enclave, actually a small corridor outfitted with three desks, a phone, a typewriter, and a mimeograph, was the Motivation "factory." This became the "M" office where an endless belt of students moved in and out, popping in for a friendly greeting, to register a complaint about some injustice, or to get hell. There was no moment in the day when the dynamic Mrs. Fel wasn't roping in a few boys and girls to try on an opera for size. Only when Aislee Hayes was meeting a typing deadline could she not be diverted from the typewriter by a student who was more attracted to her quiet but intense interest in his problem of the moment. The three of us conducted the Program, each with definitive duties but each overlapping the others' functions when she was needed, for no matter what else, the student came first. During a report period they would come. The student who was apathetic in class or unresponsive to the interstudent stimulation; the boy or girl who was bored with an unmotivated teacher or turned off with a lack of understanding as to why two angles were equal—these found their way to us for a tutor or for a "heart to heart." But it didn't have to be that kind of tête-à-tête.

Occasionally Paul Rosato came in with two or three poems he'd written last night when he should have been studying his Algebra II, or this morning in class when the teacher was asking him to participate in a discussion. This boy had such talent! His poetry was of a quality that sent me searching that evening through my contemporary poetry books, so sure was I that Paul was plagiarizing. Where had this child of a grandmother's love, a child with no father or mother, a child whose eyes had seen only the dourness of poverty, developed the artistic wisdom to see a shaft of sunlight as a "spear of gold"? Where did this brazen young Puerto Rican, mute in class, learn to string together the words of love?

> She is old, my ma, she is frail, my ma.
> She is my life, my ma, she is my love, my ma.
> My Ma? It's you, Gramma.

They used to tell the teaching staff not to touch the students. It could be dangerous for an older woman to show affection for a young man or for a male teacher to put an arm around a girl. I could understand the administration directive intellectually. But in my work, the mutual exchange of touching hands, a touch of a cheek or the hair, a mock punch at a shoulder, was often more motivational than many of society's empty words.

Paul was one of those who needed this touch. I came to love his breezing in and out of our cubicle, his swift arm around my shoulder in greeting, a new poem thrust shyly under my eyes.

I've lost Paul in these six years—one of the failures. Well, perhaps not a failure. I can't tell that, but not a success in terms of our goals. He was doing well in his senior year. He'd been accepted to a good college. Everything would be made available—tuition, room, board, spending money. Then in July, a month after graduation, his grandparents were killed in an accident. The next I heard, Paul had joined the Navy and was gone. Many, many of my "M" students have kept in touch, by phone, visit, letter. Paul is gone. I've searched in every direction. It's as if Paul never existed. I've said he was, perhaps, a failure. I continue to hope that wherever he is, if Vietnam did not become his early grave, the investment we made in his life, in his self-esteem, will have made him a happier man than he was as a child. This was one of our great goals in the Program, that a man's education should make him a happy human being, should give him the good life.

Today, I observe the fifteen "M" coordinators, cultural organizers, and secretaries in our various schools. I listen with pleasure to their "successes." A single success, I know, reflects many hours of cajoling, talking, convincing. John Knox at Bok Technical High didn't leave tailoring and enter the "M" Program as a college-bound student on an impetuous whim. Searching, Mrs. Jessie Morris, coordinator, found his brightness buried in accumulated statistics in the "iron lung." It took her days of negotiation with him and his mother before he could believe her line. Making the change, he took a giant step toward a new life.

This business of taking on the lives of others, of becoming emotionally involved in their troubles, often became a heavy burden. How does one shake off the horror of young death? I saw Charles at 2:30 one afternoon. I was never to see him again. A handsome, bright tenth-grader, Charles had left school, walked home, and entered his house to find his drunken father beating his mother. She cowered against the mantel, Charles shielding her with his big body. Enraged, Mr. B. lunged to the side and pulled down a sabre he'd brought from Korea. Quickly he plunged it into Charles's chest. I was called to give Mrs. B. solace that evening. She wanted me to tell her over and over how smart, how charming her Charles had been. Devastated by her tragedy, she nevertheless relived the hopes I had aroused in her for Charles's future. For the hundredth time I recalled the oft-spoken lie that the poor and the blacks have no interest in their children's welfare, this myth on which America's white society was bred.

We believed the "M" students needed association with the adult society to develop their personalities.

8

Summer "M" on Campus

There is much to be learned within the community. My experience tells me there is more learning to be had outside the schoolhouse than within. The techniques for making this learning available depend on the teacher's guidance and the personnel designated to "arrange for the experiences." A teacher is harassed with overcrowded classes, with disinterested and obstreperous students, with bookkeeping and sundry activities. For this reason a specially designated person must be assigned to the coordination of learning with the community. The investment for such a person will be compensated for in vast amounts by the improvement of the children's education. In the "M" Program, the cultural organizer arranges that a group of students will spend a morning observing a radio station's functions and then go to a television station to be part of the taping of a show. If the experience is especially successful for a student, the Program will arrange for the student to serve a kind of apprenticeship in the field.

James Rye was a young man who liked nothing in school except for the theater, with which he became acquainted in his ninth year. Elsie Kuhn, cultural organizer at Frankford High, arranged that he work with Dr. Sidney Bloom, the director of the Drama Guild, with whom the "M" Program carried on a very active theater project. From this point James was hooked on "the square stuff."

The cultural organizers work with teachers to provide stimulation of all kinds, which will become one with the classwork. The interrelated and independent work that the double periods provided by the roster blocking of the "M" students, facilitated study, out-of-school work and cultural experience. Since one of the Program goals was to expose the "M" students, our future leadership, to all components of our society, I felt it important that they get to know the problems of other people—the blind, deaf, orphaned, aged, etc. Acting on my arrangements with the director of the Pennsylvania School for the Deaf, Mrs. Elaine Nagler, the cultural organizer combined her Germantown High "M" students with adolescents having hearing difficulties. Together they attended ball games, dance concerts, and plays. From the association each student came away with a sympathy and a new understanding, which should be the goal of education for all.

The curriculum in the class must be the substance of life around us—the people we meet. Thus the Host Visits and the cultural experiences in which the "M" students engage are fertile fields for curriculum coordination. Seemingly we are separated from the community, but actually what happens "outside" is integral to what we learn "inside."

Mrs. Gloria Moskowitz, our cultural organizer at Bartram High, had sent fourteen students to see the Bolshoi Ballet one Sunday afternoon. It had taken a lot of talk, much discussion with students of the gymnastics involved in dance, assurance that the male dancers are real men, an appreciation of form, rhythm, meaning. After the performance four of the tall young men walked up Broad Street stimulated by the motion, the color, and the music. Their program booklets were in their hands. An old dowager type, as the boys recounted later, was walking beside them, swathed in fur, her patrician nose raised and pointing as she looked at the boys.

"Were you in the Academy?" she asked.

"Yes, we were, ma'am."

"You mean you went to see the Bolshoi?"

"Yes, we did, ma'am!"

"Why, I didn't know Negroes go to the Academy!"

"The gang we go with do! We dig it!" And a hostile lapse into black English.

Well answered. But with hurt to a newly developing pride. In 1971 to be called a Negro, to be considered unworthy of the Academy by a biased old woman! In the retelling to Mrs. M., the students got to understand human cruelty and the motivation. Despite the hurt, the incident had advanced them to a new plane. But it needed the guidance of concerned teachers to make this incident "work" for the kids.

Finally, we are living in an age in which all of life is the classroom, where every science, each social event or confrontation, is of immediate relationship to every child and man; personal experience or the media make it so. It is indeed an age in which the pulling of a tree out of the pavement to make his street wider for traffic is a threat to a child's very breath. Yet in ignorance of the whirlwind to be reaped by destruction of life around us, we continue destroying in the name of progress. The death of farmers' cows from exposure to nuclear fallout is of concern to more than SPCA groups. The sciences, mathematics, sociology, literature, art—all must be understood and taught as the humanities, for all are related completely and organically to the mind and body of a human being. We are one, with all time and all humanity joined in our very atoms, as Dr. Osol had said to our "M" students in their summer program. All exist through the being of those before. The moon walk could not have happened without Einstein, who could not have taken his gigantic step without Newton, who needed Galileo, who based his findings on Copernicus. We are the sum of all knowledge, interrelated knowledge.

And central to all is the teacher—despite an old belief that "you cannot teach a man anything; you can only help him to find it within himself." Despite this, it is the teacher with his wider and perhaps wiser experience who must lead the child to himself and to the finding of knowledge. It is the teacher who, while making learning fun, must get children to "dig" the necessity for developing skill in certain areas when it is non-fun activity. This, too, is the role of the teacher who has been appointed by society to prepare children for the experiences of life. And this is what we must create—superlative teachers—out of the average, normal human beings into whose care we give our treasure.

Creative enthusiasm is catching in a school. But the climate must be established and nurtured by the principal. If he wills it, encourages it, supervises it, his teachers and counselors will knock themselves out trying to achieve. Of course it's all for the most charitable reasons, for the children. But as we know and the staff knows, this kind of self-stimulation or motivation makes life livable, makes the dreariest morning challenging and a deskful of papers at night an acceptable part of the job.

Although the coordinator was the person who made the Motivation machine run, I was operating the project as the principal's idea man and officer-in-charge. It is the principal in every case who has to promote his professional ideas. It is he who must provide strong leadership. His philosophy of life and education, his ability to understand the needs and potential of his staff and students, his capacity to motivate all groups toward positive action will either make or break his school operation. In today's climate of mounting community concern there is no middle ground. The principal must produce. But it becomes increasingly difficult to do so in the face of many pressures, overcrowding, community demands, racial conflicts, often unreasonable union demands. Despite these difficult problems, the principal must be permitted to serve his school as its leader and supervisor. The needs of his students and staff are more important than any event outside his building. He must not be used as a public relations man. Teachers who know that the boss is interested in what they are doing in class will want to perform and grow. Students who know the principal is around watching and advising will show confidence in the school. The principal sets the climate.

In the "M" story, the majority of high school principals using the Motivation Program saw this as an alternative educational experience for the few hundred students in their own schools who had been traditionally short-changed. In those schools the desires of the principals, the strong leadership they provided, gave the "M" coordinators the support and authority on which to build a well-structured program. In three of the fifteen schools the program is not functioning healthily. It is clearly because the principals have not exerted the kind of strong support and leadership necessary to overcome the cynicism of "those who know what's best for the students." In each case, with weak direction, monies and efforts have been dissipated. This kind of unconcerned, tepid leadership has plagued and destroyed many excellent programs throughout the country. The children are the losers.

The principal who involves himself in every project in his school, to whatever extent he can, is providing real leadership which stimulates everyone on his staff. His coming to one preview to listen to a discussion after the film gives him a new insight into what thought is going into his "M" Program and curriculum. A principal who comes to one of the Open Talk Groups or an "M" Parents meeting has learned that the "M" Program has instruments for communication between the generations that will help his students move ahead without conflict. The principal who knows that talk and negotiation lead to peace and productivity in his school will encourage this kind of continual talk. But the principal who fears talk must be ready to face confrontation, a bellicose act which, even when it is verbal, cannot lead to peace and to a school climate in which children will feel secure and learn.

Finally, the principal's personality, his experience, his observation and support, are the center of life of the entire school, but most especially of the "M" Program, since he soon sees the beneficial contagion spreading to the larger school community.

In those first five years of the Program, I prepared three "M" summer programs as potential models. They were given on the campuses of the Philadelphia College of Pharmacy and Science and the University of Pennsylvania. Each summer, over two hundred of the "M" students spent six weeks in a college atmosphere, studying how to think, to listen, to speak and read, to write compositions, outlines, and term papers. It was a breathless six weeks. No one received credit for the summer, nor did they ask for it. This was voluntary attendance. The upperclassmen, the "M" seniors, took a prep course to be ready for college. But by far the most popular course was the unit I had prepared for my humanities curriculum, "The Ethnic Backgrounds of the American People." By this time the Program had been installed in thirteen other high schools. This "Ethnic" course, then, had a mélange of "M" students—Asian, Kalmuck, Ukrainian, Polish, Irish, Italian, black, and Jewish. The course of study consisted of seven books representing various ethnic writers, the writings of sociologists, hours of discussions comparing the lives of Americans, hours of uprooting and destroying stereotypical bias. In evaluation one student wrote that he had learned more in the six weeks than in eleven years of school.

One of the most rewarding features in the course was the presentation, twice each week, of lectures by community leaders who represented the ethnic groups being studied. Each lecturer discussed his people's problems as immigrants and their problems today. The "M" students plied the speaker with questions. Many of these adults, whom I'd selected for their special qualities, left permanent and beneficent impressions on their young audience.

One of our lecturers was Matthew Costanzo, who was director of junior high schools for the School District. This young gentleman, one generation removed from the same Italian immigrants the two hundred students had just studied in Jerre Mangione's beautiful story of Italian-American life, "Mount Allegro," provided a singular bond, a relationship with his young audience. He and they had both experienced personal and social hardships; and look! He'd made it! Later he was to become superintendent of the School District of Philadelphia.

George Hutt, one of the early community supporters of the "M" Program, was now one of two black members of the Board of Education of Philadelphia. He well understood the problems of his young audience. He'd never forgotten his own poverty and self-deprecation. He'd been a high school dropout and a wanderer. Nevertheless, despite the impossible odds, he'd finished engineering school at Drexel University. A militant, disenchanted with the educational system, he became a Board member to help effect change. He wouldn't believe in a program until he'd seen it. He had watched the "M" Program since its beginning at West Philadelphia High in 1963 and he was convinced we meant business for the children.

His coming as the lecturer was an event for the two hundred students. He was known to them. They took pride in his being a Board member. He was warm and affectionate. He told the audience what he'd lived through, the self-hatred, the discrimination he had experienced, and how it had motivated him instead of destroying him. He spoke not only of what had gone before but of what they should expect of America in the future in civil rights, education, in living. He had them going, that audience. Even the non-blacks were inspired with his exhortations that all of them had to fight to make a good society. They had to grab the help being given them in the "M" Program and make the best of themselves. The kids were delighted with his good looks, his youth, and his inner fire.

In the question period, Cecelia raised her hand. She had rarely found the courage to participate in the questioning of the lecturers, although she was a vocal participant after they'd left the lecture hall to return to the classroom. She was almost seventeen, very dark, and not especially attractive; but she was a lovely young woman who had taken hold in her eleventh year and had fallen in love with history, especially the history of the Negroes.

"Mr. Hutt," she called out timidly, "what is your idea of Negro beauty?"

The lecturer looked down from the platform at the young woman whose black eyes seemed to be glowing. With no hesitation he answered, "My idea of Negro beauty? Someone just like you!"

Cecelia is in her third year of college. She will be a social studies teacher. She told me recently that his response that summer was the most significant thing that had ever happened to her as a woman. It had helped her to change her personality. A man had seen beauty in her.

Among many stimulating speakers that summer, Dr. Arthur Osol, president of the Philadelphia College of Pharmacy and Science, was one of the best. Having worked through six weeks studying the unreliability of stereotypes, our "M" students sat before this handsome, well-dressed, white-haired Main Liner wondering what he could possibly know about ethnic problems. He had probably come over with the *Mayflower*. This was the general assessment as Dr. Osol took over the lectern.

With his first few sentences, he proved how ludicrous were widely held stereotypes. He was born in Lithuania and was brought to America as a young child of a minority group. He was terribly poor but managed, over the years, to overcome the disabilities of immigrant poverty, as had many others. Many of his friends, he added, had never been able to surmount it. He had become a physicist and a professor, and now, in his sixties, he was president of the Philadelphia College of Pharmacy and Science.

He spoke as a physicist about the physical oneness of contemporary mankind with man in the eons of the past; that every breath inhaled and exhaled contained the atoms of the man who breathed 10,000 years ago as much as it contained the atoms of the breath of the boy in the next seat. Dr. Osol, the patrician, Lithuanian-born American physicist, impressed upon the multi-ethnic Motivation audience a most important fact: that we are indivisible and totally a part of each other.

These were a few of the inputs from the community that were significant in the learning and development of our "M" students. What they received from the outside world helped them understand the kinds of change needed in the school curriculum. They saw the need for new and dynamic education that would bring them closer to the world in which they were living and in which they would raise the next generation.

On the other hand, the community developed a new sense of its importance to the young and their education and to the kinds of physical involvement needed of them.

This Summer Motivation Institute gave the students another activity which made them understand that they were integral to the life of the community as well as to their families. If the students wished, they could take part in the Open Talk Sessions with our psychologist, Dr. Sara Taubin, as leader. The students and their parents met with Dr. Taubin to discuss normal teenagers' problems. In seven sessions both generations were helped to learn ways of avoiding conflict, ways to negotiate the normal problems of the age.

I wanted the "M" students to be willing to look at themselves as they are when alone, with the family, at school, with people in general. I felt that if they could see themselves and be willing to "mark" themselves they would then be able to take the steps that would mean improvement. Dr. Taubin and I prepared two personal inventory forms(pp. 126 ff.), including a daily inventory based on a game I had played in my own high-school days. The two hundred "M" students of the Summer Institute kept their inventories faithfully, surprising themselves and us with the degree of self-improvement.

The interesting results the students obtained with their inventories in the summer weeks gave them and us some fascinating perceptions about a person's unwillingness to verbalize and objectify his faults. It was both painful and pleasant for the students to have to keep a daily tally for such items as: "Do I like myself better?" and "I have done the following today to come closer to one goal." The daily personal inventory served as a guide to the student for increasing his motivation. Completing this inventory meant really facing the problem and handling it. The Open Talk Sessions that Dr. Taubin conducted in conjunction with the summer programs were tremendously valuable to students and parents. She brought to the sessions her vast experience and expertise with family and adolescent behavior and was able to provide the "M" families with good techniques for the resolution of normal problems.

SCHOOL DISTRICT OF PHILADELPHIA
MOTIVATION PROGRAM
SUMMER INSTITUTE

GENERAL PERSONAL INVENTORY

SELF-APPRAISAL

The good things about myself now are:

___

Some things about myself that need to be improved are:

___

GETTING ALONG WITH OTHERS

Family
The good things between me and my family are:

___

My family and I would get along better if

___

School
School is satisfying in the following ways:

___

But I would get more out of school if

___

Friends
When I think about having friends, the good things they mean to me are:

___

The problems I have with friendships are:

___

People in general
I like people who

___

I dislike people who

___

Goals

This summer. I would like to accomplish the following goals during the time of the Summer Institute:

___

During high school. My goals for my high school education are:

___

Long-range goals. In addition, I have long-range educational goals, which include:

___

Motivation. I am stimulated to work toward my goals under the following circumstances:

INCREASED MOTIVATION THROUGH PERSONAL CHANGE

(I know I can become motivated if I can change in some ways, both small and large.)
This summer I hope to change in the following ways:

During my high school years I believe I can change my life pattern in such ways as:

A longer time may be needed, but I know I will mature in these additional areas:

Some things that are not likely to change are:

If some of the following things could happen, I could improve my motivation to grow to my fullest potential, personally, as a family member, in school, and in the community:

SCHOOL DISTRICT OF PHILADELPHIA
MOTIVATION PROGRAM
SUMMER INSTITUTE

DAILY PERSONAL INVENTORY

Enter a plus (+) or a minus (−) each day.

	July											August					
	13	14	17	18	19	20	21	24	25	26	27	28	31	1	2	3	4	7	8
Do I look better today?																			
Do I feel better today?																			
Am I getting along better at home?																			
Am I getting along better in school?																			
Did I strive to achieve my best?																			
Am I getting along better with people?																			
Have I more self-respect due to my thoughts and actions?																			
Do I like myself better?																			
Do I have the support and respect of people around me?																			

I have done the following today to come closer to one goal:

(Example: <u>I have approached a friend.</u>)

Date   Item

_____   _____

> We found that anxiety interfered with the "M" student's learning. Warm support about his ability, his looks, his personality, often allayed his anxiety.

9

The Environment for Motivation

Benjy was yet another type, of another ethnic group, whose motivational problems stemmed from sources different from the majority in the early "M" Program. He was Jewish, the son of bright, artistic parents who wanted the best for their two sons. The boys grew up with books, music, theater, and good talk. Above all, they were surrounded by the love their parents showered on them. All the ingredients for a well-motivated, happy personality existed and yet something went wrong in Benjy's first year at Central, the prestigious academic school at the other end of the city. He became a nervous, trembling adolescent whose thoughts came out in stutters, and inexorably, as the year wore on, his studying habits and marks deteriorated. No amount of talking to him or teachers shed light on the problem. He had stopped eating properly and was sleeping poorly. He was seeing nothing of former friends but would come home and shut himself in his room. There he read and reread, over and over, his favorite books. By the end of the year he was finding every excuse to stay away from school. So now everyone knew it was something to do with school.

His parents had investigated the "M" Program at West Philadelphia High, which was three years old, and by September, Benjy was enrolled. The Program had succeeded in attracting back 13 percent white students, whereas the rest of the school had 3 percent whites. So Benjy was not a lone Caucasian. Nevertheless it made little difference, since he had played with children of different ethnic groups all during his growing up in University City.

From the first week in the Program he began taking more interest in life about him, and the interest held. Florence Rose's counseling door was always open to him for any reason he saw fit to offer. If he attended a Host Visit the evening before, he stopped in to tell me about it and then went to her office to spill some of the ideas that had been discussed. He was studying better. He took up with his former friends who were also in the Program. They studied together and attended cultural events in each other's company. Each student stimulated the other. Benjy was still very quiet in class, however, and in preparation for our monthly "M" teacher meeting, I added his name to the list of "discussed students." I felt he would benefit from our concerted discussion. Everyone agreed he was bright and would become a fine student if he continued as he was going. It was Mrs. Macauley, his English teacher, who gave us the clue to his problem and the possible cure.

"He's afraid to talk in class. If he has to answer, he peers around almost furtively to see what the others are thinking. Occasionally he gets so nervous his stutter takes eight seconds to unlock. But give him a sheet of paper and can he write!"

"You mean it seriously, Helen? Really talented?"

"I mean talented! His imagery, his sensitivity are wonderful. If we can unlock it for him!"

That was the answer, and Helen Macauley started a creative writing magazine, which we opened to the entire school. Benjy was asked to be the editor. Of course he was also a major contributor and his work was of unusual maturity and merit. His last two years at West moved uneventfully but successfully to an end, a happy end. His stutter disappeared. Where had it originated? It came about because of the intense, frightening competition he met at Central. He wasn't capable, he felt. The more frightened he became, the less he could do, the more he stuttered. His recitations in many classes were so disjointed that students laughed at him, and—whether imagined or not—the teachers simply passed over him. His self-esteem was low. He'd never be as talented as his older brother. Everything conspired to make him completely nonfunctional.

Life at West Philadelphia High was different, he told us. Almost every teacher he had in the Program gave him special attention. He felt happy coming to me and to the counselor. All the activities Mrs. Fel sent him to were fun. Just going with the other kids was fun even if some of the events were dull. Almost two years were lost out of Benjy's life with the threat of permanent emotional incapacity. But the individual attention of the Motivation Program had given him back his self-esteem, that most vital of all human needs.

Benjy took a scholarship to the University of Pennsylvania and has been a happy scholar for four years studying literature and writing with several inspiring professors. Often during his college years he has brought me some of his writings, not as a braggart but in a spirit of confidence that I will be honest with him. Benjy will be a great writer, I believe. Perhaps his unhappy early experience and his finding himself will be of much value in his understanding of character motivation.

I stated early in this book that I had found motivational problems the same over the world. Setting, climate, language, mores —all could be different but people were the same.

Frequently when I have worked with American Friends Service Committee organizations and when I serve as consultant to suburban community groups, I use Benjy's story to touch more intimately the minds and experiences of non-poverty populations. As I speak with them about human apathy or nonmotivation, they relate my concepts to their own growing-up problems with their parents, siblings, peers, or teachers. They examine themselves more honestly in their actions with their mates and their children. And they apply what I am saying about self-esteem and caring to our national behavior toward our fellow

The Environment for Motivation

Americans. They can see that each of us is an accumulation of many attitudes and experiences; that affluence is not an antidote to the problems that beset a personality; that, in fact, affluence might exacerbate the damage to the human being. The most serious message I try to leave them, as with all the "M" Parents Groups and teachers I see throughout the city, is that taking active measures to build self-esteem and to show that the child is loved will build up the child's defenses against the many outside pressures he will have to withstand in his growing years.

Teachers have also found new motivation through their involvement with the "M" Program. One who underwent such a change was Stephen White, a shop teacher at West Philadelphia High School. Stephen White came from a poor Irish immigrant family where a good part of the pay envelope was spent in the saloon before it reached the house. His childhood remained in his mind as a nightly and Sunday yelling brawl. His eyes saw the banging around of his mother and the seven kids. Stephen left school in the eleventh grade to take a job hauling dirt on the same construction job where his father worked. It was backbreaking work. He froze in winter and blistered in summer. And what did he have left at the end of the week? Nothing. He hated it—working with the jigs and the wops. God they stank! There was only one decent wop. That was the foreman. He'd taken a liking to Steve, or maybe the dago was just taking advantage of his young legs. It didn't matter to Steve. It interrupted the shoveling of the dirt and gave him a chance to run from the site to the builder's hut. One thing he loved was running. Would he like to run in track! He could also get away from his father on these errands. Boy, how he hated that stinkin' drunk. It was on one of these errands that all the hates, the loves, and the secret hopes that a man needs met their moment of motivation.

Each time Steve entered the warm hut, breathing hard as he sprinted from the site in the cold air, he brought the foreman's papers to a boy his own age working at a desk piled high with ledgers and an adding machine. Steve remembered the guy from his own class in high school. He was a Jew and Steve never bothered with the Christ-killers. But Ben was one of the nice ones, he remembered. He had gotten some tutoring in math from him in the tenth grade. Not that he needed much; he was pretty good in math. Always was. And here was Ben, the builder's bookkeeper.

"I see you're still running," Ben said one day. "You're good. Shame you didn't stay on the team. It sure went down when you quit school."

"Hey, Ben, how'd ya get the job? Ya the boss's son or somethin'?"

"Hell, no," Ben answered. "After graduation, I went from builder to builder until I got this. And I go to night school at Temple for accounting. Hey, why'd ya drop out? Need the money?"

"One of the reasons. What did I have to stay for, to get the same job?"

"You were good in math. Ya could've gotten the same thing I have. Hey, why'n't ya go back and get your diploma?"

That was the beginning. Steve took night courses, got the high school diploma and decided immediately that he'd like to take night courses at Temple just as Ben was doing. In the meantime he was learning some electrical jobs, picking them up wherever he could as an apprentice. At the end of the year he decided to enter Temple full time. He was on the track team. He thought maybe he could be a teacher. During the summer he made his pile of dough on the job sites, now that he was in the union. The hardest part was being on the team with the jigs, although he had to admit there were two of them he'd gotten to like. He was getting used to the Jews, too.

When he was graduated he entered the school system as a shop teacher in electricity. I got to know him when he'd already been at West several years. He was becoming less interested in his classes as they became largely black.

I found him an attractive man for all his bias. He found me an attractive woman despite my being Jewish. The "M" office was on the same side of the building as his shop. He'd stop down occasionally to talk about the teachers' union we were anxious to get started. We'd been around a long time and had seen the kind of repression and discrimination practiced on disenfranchised teachers. It was time for a union.

Every time he came into the "M" office he was exposed to the "new breed." This was what I called my "M" flock. They were to be the leadership. The more I talked, the more they believed. At first Steve thought I was pretty funny with all that talk; funny and unfair to lead these kids and their parents down the garden path. Since it was too early for any kind of data, all I could give him was talk, philosophy, and subjective demonstrations. Occasionally he'd admit to some of my findings. Secretly I could see him undergoing a subtle change. His attitude toward the students was much less often infected by deprecating patronage. He ignored them less frequently. He was engaging in a normal association, normal chatting.

Finally, he asked me if I were willing to expose some of my "M" students to an electricity club. I jumped at the chance. I couldn't have constructed a better project myself. Indeed, the combination of academic and vocational training for all students had long been my ideal. The project was undertaken. Steve had become a highly motivated teacher, excited by the "romance" of his subject and the possibilities to be achieved by the "M" students. I am certain that this experience was responsible for the great changes in Steve as a teacher and a person. He became active in our program as a chaperone and frequently came along on bus trips. He saw the students as people now, and his change elicited new relationships not only with "M" students but with his regular, nonacademic trade-prep classes.

In the years since I have directed the "M" Program for the city, Steve became the successful coordinator of one of the fifteen Programs. Now he has moved up and become an administrator in establishing a new high school. He pleases me greatly, for much of what he has brought into being is a direct reflection of what he has overcome in his own background and what he has learned about people, all people, and their motivation.

The teacher does not have to love her students but she must care for their success. Her sincerity and honesty will help achieve it.

10
Teachers Are Human

Since a student is a product of his environment, his motivation must derive from it too. We felt, in the "M" Program, that all elements of our society need this motivation: students, parents, community. And central to the entire process of education is, I believe, the motivation of the teacher. On this person's motivation depends the development of our children.

Two years ago as I was walking in West Philadelphia I caught sight of a woman's figure some distance away, and the swivel of her hips gave me a throwback to my early childhood. With the visual recognition came a feeling of queasiness, a reaction that occasionally accompanied some emotional distress. I ran breathlessly to catch up to this person and as I came abreast of her I looked her full in the face. It was Miss Holly! My Miss Holly who had been my second-grade teacher in Vare Elementary School, forty-five years before. Her tall angular body was thinner and bent, her black hair now white, her beady, piercing brown eyes dulled with age, her mouth thin and taut, bitter, a face gnarled like a diseased tree trunk, but it was my Miss Holly. I felt a sudden hatred, a fear; and just as suddenly, I laughed aloud as I felt a release from the ancient dread.

So lasting is the teacher's influence over the child, so deep an impression does a person make that it is frightening to consider the responsibility that we grant the teachers of our children without providing them with proper training, an understanding of people and of life around them. My role as coordinator of the Motivation Program provided me with a fine observation post from which I could observe the immediate results of varied teacher style and behavior, and the lack of intelligent and relevant training.

In this profession one leaves the cloister of liberal arts or a school of education in which neither the discipline nor the art of teaching was learned well, if at all. One puts the books on the shelf to rest there, *ad aeternum,* and the ill-prepared teaching candidate is thrust into the classroom. Until recently teachers of parochial schools needed only their own high school diplomas in order to teach. The teacher is often caught in a difficult school situation, for she may be just a few years older than the students themselves. By what method should she convey the material to those before her? How should she get them to sit still and remain quiet? Before she is aware of it, her personality has become a scolding, anxious one, and damage to the learning child has begun.

It isn't entirely that the teacher is unprepared to be a teacher that does the damage. It is the fact that the teacher is often not prepared to be a human being, an example of a human to her class of thirty-five children, whom she will see for 190 days that year. This is the man or woman who will convey to the children humaneness, sympathy, understanding, judgment, morality, or the antitheses of all of these.

In the second grade my Miss Holly ridiculed the Jewish children, the Italians and the one Negro boy. She gave her judgment on each group of immigrants who had infested her white, Anglo-Saxon, Protestant world. It was the only thing that gave her any satisfaction, although if she had been confronted with such lowly thoughts, she would have rejected them as being unprofessional. Nevertheless, to a class of thirty-five immigrant children she personified the evil witch in the flesh. The year, as I remember it over all these decades, was somber, one overcast by a pall of fear and shame. I was a Jew and all Jews were loud and pushy and stingy. I was a very fat child, therefore I was a pig. The wops came in for their share. Wops had many degrading characteristics—they were greasy and smelly, they were Popish—was there anything worse?

But poor Jeremy, the lone Negro, was most humiliated by the "witch's" mouth. With a leer she pointed to the cowering boy who was close to tears, deriding the lazy niggers, their dirty houses and clothes, saying they should stay in the South where they belong. This was in 1922, when there were relatively few blacks in the North, most of these having been there for many generations. In fact, many blacks of Philadelphia had been there since before the American Revolution. But Miss Holly went at the boy again and again. "So lazy, so shiftless, even their dogs follow them around dragging themselves shiftlessly." That was funny, I thought in my seven-year-old mind, Jeremy isn't shiftless—whatever that meant—and his dog wasn't either. It wasn't a good thing to be; that I knew. But the shame, the sneer, the leer, the hurt, the tears remained with me for almost a half century. What could I have learned in that year under those conditions? What did her personality do to mine and the other children year after year?

Another year stands out in my early childhood education. I remember Mrs. Franklin in fourth grade at Vare. The year is alive in my memory with the sound of laughing, Mrs. Franklin's and ours. I have a kinesthetic memory of walking around and doing, not shrinking in the row after row of desks. I can transfer to my present a feeling of happiness that pervaded that period of my childhood. That was the year the class of ghetto children had their intellects expanded by the excitement of geography, history, commerce, and travel. I remain excited with these topics even today. One of our projects was to select some foreign country on the map, to learn everything about it. I selected Spain. It might have been the picture of a costume that attracted me. I learned about the country thoroughly. It remains clearly in my mind that I walked the seven or eight blocks to the docks on the Delaware River and asked until I found a freighter from Spain.

Mrs. Franklin had so inspired us with a need to know, with the excitement of learning, that I approached the captain of the freighter asking him what kinds of things his ship brought from Spain to America. He had a shipload of wool and cork. He had thousands and thousands of pounds of tissue-thin cork. What did it come from? Trees. What was it for? Insulation. What was that? To put in ice boxes to keep the cold in and the heat out. The captain spoke in a broken English, but he understood me and was amused. He broke open two crates and I left the ship with samples of raw wool and tissue-thin sheets of cork for my notebook. I recall walking home with jubilation, and I recall the pride with which I prepared the specimens in my notebook. That was the kind of learning I should have had from kindergarten through college. That is the essence of the teaching profession, which potential teachers should learn and often do not.

In this chapter I want to stay as closely as possible to the topic of the teacher himself, although his subject matter is intimately interwined with what he is and how he conveys the material. (I shall find myself interchanging she and he: she, because the great majority of teachers are female; he, because I wish there were more of them.) The teacher, then, is the vehicle for learning transmission. He is the agent who jostles the natural curiosity of a person. Are all teachers motivated individuals?

Recently a questionnaire to teachers concerning teacher motivation elicited this angry response from one woman: "Teachers do not need motivating. They are motivated just by becoming teachers!" Are teachers then different from all other people? Are they not products of their environments, their genetic endowment? Is their daily behavior not influenced by illness, sleepless nights, financial concerns, the disease of ethnic hatred? Was the teacher's personality not formed in childhood perhaps, by some injury to the self-esteem? Might she, therefore, not have sustained a chronic dose of apathy?

If the teacher is the transmitter of the culture and of learning, she is also the conveyor of bias and negative attitudes. She is a reflection of her own early learning and her society. Americans hold the teacher in low esteem and consider their teachers fair game to be treated in a discriminatory manner. Teachers are expected to accept these indignities in the name of dedicated professionalism. Indeed, many teachers lend themselves to the game. Often they disdain the union which has brought them a decent salary, dignity, and power. But on a relatively low salary —given five to six years of university education—the teacher is expected to raise a family, live well, and be an exponent of the social graces. She must be a paragon of virtue when in fact she is a product of an imperfect and unvirtuous society. Her personal problems and those of life around her are deposited into her personality. The teacher is, simply, a human being as imperfect as the rest of us. We imperfect people have received imperfect college preparation in the art of conveying our culture to the next generation. Thus, from generation to generation, the art of teaching and the joy of learning is lost in a maze.

Every year a new crop of idealistic young graduates complete their practice teaching and take a full-time job. They are eager, spending hours preparing visual aids, bright posters, paste ups. The first few weeks are a joy for the new teacher. But gradually the excitement wears off. Thirty-five children are too many to keep enchanted all day. The techniques she has learned at college just don't do the job. At the end of a few months her job has become "teaching school," not "teaching children." The mass situation, the mass problems, the lack of administrative cooperation, and some private attitudes all add up to failure. By the end of the first year many young teachers seek other employment. What is wrong? Why are teachers unprepared for the problems they meet?

In an effort to embrace the total intellectual life of the country, becoming the dispensers of certification, the colleges have continued year after year to practice the mystic rites of the schools of education. From the early '20s and '30s, when "education courses" were undergraduate and unproductive, to the present, when teacher-manufacturing is graduate-level, the product has been fairly even—that is, far less than satisfactory. The courses are directly out of the whalebone corset era. The lecturers frequently demonstrate that they not only have never been near an urban classroom but clearly have no concept of the city schools' comprehensive problems. College students are still doing their practice teaching in suburban schools but must come to the city market for their jobs.

The university that trains a doctor to treat human physical ailments, that trains a lawyer to service man through the laws of the state, still prepares the teacher, the conveyor of the culture, the developer of the citizenry, in a most imperfect manner. Until recent years medical schools excluded their students from any humanities courses. The humanities weren't considered necessary for the practice of medicine. More recently, progressive medical schools have merged the humanities and medicine. The teacher, too, a fair copy of society, must be sensitized, developed intellectually, and given an understanding of human needs while she is learning her academic discipline. The latter is less important, I believe, than the familiarity with people and a knowledge of how they are affected by their environment.

If the university is to prepare our teachers, it must send them out of the college and expose them early and fully to life with young students. Their internship, working with master teachers, must cover the entire period while they are also developing their academic expertise and their ability to influence the behavior of a class.

Young teachers should be exposed to the idea that as teachers they must continue to grow intellectually as well as humanely. Their exit from the university classroom should be the beginning of a life of self-development not only in their own subject but in all areas of learning. This intellectuality would provide a teacher with the breadth of cultural development that would make her worthy of her title. A personal exposure to culture on a broad scale would endow the teacher with the learning style she would need to deal with multiple problems over the years. But it is the university that must implant the pattern in the teacher candidate if the growth is to become permanent and salutary.

The college has the same responsibility in the professional development of guidance counselors. I have observed over many years that (if it is possible) the universities do a less satisfactory job of preparing the counselor than of preparing the teacher. There are few standards or qualifications for entering this delicate school profession. With some notable and brilliant exceptions, many counselors I work with were unsuccessful in the classroom and so bring some strong bias into this role, which requires the most sensitive human contact. Like too many teachers, many of the counselors end all intellectual growth when they return their mortar boards. Their emotional sensitivity, vis-à-vis their young clients, develops a *rigor mortis* in direct proportion to the amount of record keeping they must do.

I lay the responsibility for ineffective teacher and counselor preparation in the lap of the universities. The problem is not that they are not capable of the job, but that they do not have the will and thus the creativity. I believe the day is not far off when the large school districts will undertake the preparation of their own teachers, counselors, and administrators. They, the school personnel, will learn on the job. Then the universities can provide the citizens and school personnel with the cultural scholarship germane to a university's purpose.

Since I think of "intellectual growth" as a continuing familiarity with the humanities, I have urged this teaching vehicle on many Motivation teachers over the years. Each year, more "M" teachers report in our seminars that the use of the humanities promotes stimulation and continued education of the teacher. Thus she is provided with constant fueling and refueling helping her to maintain what I have called "the romance of her subject." It has pleased me over the years to find many bland personalities who have become inspired and exciting teachers because of their scholarship and intellectual curiosity. With scholarship and intellectual curiosity a teacher can stimulate and create excitement in the classroom. It is an almost impossible feat for a teacher who is excited with her discipline to project a dull lesson. The very spark that motivates the teacher to continue growing with the subject will also spark the apathetic class and student.

This was the kind of teacher I wanted for the early Motivation Program at West Philadelphia High. We were indeed lucky to have had many such. In the fifteen programs today, for teachers who want to be creative, there are many opportunities to try out new ideas within a well-structured project.

We were a demanding program asking that all involved be willing to give their utmost. The teachers knew the college goals and how much had to be done with the "M" students to prepare them, to overcome the undereducation they had.

Cecil Richardson, "Si," taught English to our "M" students and to those of Drexel University as well. He exemplified the British "don." Our students who had Si in class had the privilege of having a sensitive human being who cared for them and who was also a great teacher of literature. Shakespeare's *Macbeth,* as Si taught it, was a living, human experience, not simply an antique play. He never talked down to the students. His discussion with them about human motivation, greed, ambition, Lady Macbeth's life during sleep, were worthy of a college class. His goals were high. He never downgraded. What he asked for was simply part of his course and his concept of their ability to perform. The bell at the end of the period was an intrusion for the "M" students and for Si, for he was an enthusiastic "M" teacher.

I don't want to give the impression that I think a teacher must be an intellectual giant to be effective. A fellow student with a bit more information can do all that is needed in a tutoring situation. An amateur, a neighbor, may be an excellent teacher. The vital ingredient is the chemistry that exists between the teacher and class, his attitude toward their abilities, their persons, his self-motivation and his own continued intellectual development.

Don Warner had the kind of chemistry that drew "M" students to enroll in his "M" summer school without reward of marks or credit. This black, handsome, soft-spoken man with his Marine background seemed out of place in an English class. But his training worked for him and the kids. He refused shoddy work and insisted on the best. No matter how many times the composition had to be redone, it had to be the student's best. Sweating over a paragraph that hot summer in an effort to achieve comprehension, the students might have thrown it up and taken off. No. They came day after day for six weeks because Mr. Warner made them feel as they had never felt before. It wasn't only the blacks who felt this strength and approval from Don Warner. The white student, the brilliant but lazy student, the average but striving student, all received his mental caress and his encouragement. Don was the first "M" coordinator at Bartram High School when the Program was opened. After a few years he became a vice-principal. Today he is the principal of a high school in a New Jersey city. It is a tribute to the judgment of the board of education of that city that they could perceive those elements of humaneness that had made him an excellent "M" teacher and administrator, and that they imported him to administer their suburban school.

We saw in the Program that a concerned teacher could become a concerned and excellent coordinator in one of the fifteen high schools; and that if he provided the same kind of involvement in this job, the students' chances of success were excellent. Miss Dena Obus was this kind of teacher and coordinator.

Charlotte Evans was a loner mainly because she was always depressed, was physically unattractive, and had a strong odor about her. Her fellow students left her alone. Teachers talked about the girl. Finally Miss Obus became aware of the trouble. She brought Charlotte in day after day, ostensibly to have her help in the office. They shared laughter and Cokes. They shared childhood tales. At last it came out. Charlotte had constant pain in her side. Miss Obus persuaded Charlotte to go with her to the doctor and the hospital. The young woman had a fatal kidney disease. She needed to trust someone who showed concern for her.

A teacher who possesses this natural warmth and regard for students will never use criticism to produce shame. On the contrary, a teacher using praise and encouragement can give the student enough self-confidence so that he can admit occasional failure or noncompetence and seek help. If the student has the same kind of support at home, he will probably enjoy a healthy personality development. More frequently parents are too preoccupied to offer praise. A perceptive teacher can in small measure overcome this parental slight.

Recently I attended an ecology seminar. I moved slowly in the line to a table to register. As I took up the pen to write, I looked into the warm, brown eyes of an elderly lady and I felt a surge of memory and pleasure. "Miss Masland?" I asked quietly. "Yes," she answered with the same happy smile I had responded to a hundred times. "You were one of my most wonderful teachers at Girls'." I told her my maiden name, as if she would remember thirty-eight years of girls who had passed by. It poured out, just as it used to do. I responded to her because I wanted to please her, to have her praise and smile. It wasn't the mark in history. It would be A or B. That didn't matter. It was her stimulation of the class, that smile she was sharing with me this minute. "Rebecca"—she held my hand—"you've made this a special day for me." I felt the same reward I had felt as an adolescent.

Not all teacher-student relationships have an emotional reward. Perhaps few do. But there must be a reward of some kind. Ours is a reward-punishment society, and it is thus that our values are established. Furthermore, the student must understand failure, since reward, punishment, and failure are components of life. The students must learn to "handle" these often uncomfortable conditions.

Mrs. Phyllis Wirtshafter is a social studies teacher who taught one of the "M" Summer Institutes. She wrote in her evaluation that the free, intellectual stimulation provided her by the students who had suddenly learned it was fun to learn, gave her the most enjoyable experience in twenty-five years of teaching. It was a revealing statement, coming from an exciting teacher. As for reward, the students found it in their own pleasure and achievement.

One of the serious demands we made of our "M" teachers was that they make preparation for immediate and long-range goals. I was particularly bothered by teachers of all ages who wanted to be their students' buddies. They felt that this kind of warmth was needed. That was fine, except that in the process the teacher forgot the goals of the Program and what the students needed to accumulate academically. The teachers "played." Every day was communication time. "What shall we talk about today?" was the opening aria every day. From this, hours of "rapping" would ensue, which might have had some merit. Nevertheless, the skills needed for the students' future were overlooked. At the same time, the teacher was remarkably free from evening composition papers. When we discovered this type of "unstructured" teacher, she was advised and helped in her preparation. Curriculum was suggested. Finally if the teacher did not change, her roster was changed. This free-school style is not within our model.

In our Program, we evaluated every project we undertook in terms of the payoff for the students. What would they get out of it? Not only the project went through the test; each staff person and his role had to meet the same qualifications. How, we asked, would this project or person stimulate thought, language, and activity? Yet often we were hamstrung by personnel at every level: administration, department head, teacher or union fears.

Our young people had much in common no matter whether they'd come from a poverty or middle-class background. They were all unmotivated, nonreading products of the television age. Most had families where both parents or the only parent worked. The evenings were not a time for family togetherness. There was little communication or discussion of news, world affairs, or of oneself. So we were all pretty much the same. Nobody was dying to get to school. But we'd all experienced and seen games that "grab the kids."

Early in the West Philadelphia "M" Program, we'd planned the seven additional English and math periods to give them more literature, more discussion and work with college boards. The math periods were intended to develop concepts. Remedial work was to be undertaken by the tutoring project. Much depended on the teacher. If he were creative and believed in the students' abilities they benefited by an exciting and sophisticated curriculum. We knew we had to enlarge our young peoples' intellects by the enriched classes. The "M" students were exposed to enriched science, math, social studies, English, and foreign language classes. They had to meet the competition they would meet first in the college board exams and then in their college classes. In the English periods, much of the individual teacher's curriculum was devised by herself with guidance from Henry Weisberg, our department head.

Between 1966 and 1969 urban schools throughout the country were embroiled in the problem of black studies. By 1967, our Negro friends wanted to be black. Even the "M" classes struggled to maintain an ethnic balance. There was dignity and beauty in blackness. There was relevance and great interest in black subjects. Nothing mattered but black subjects. Some schools which were 100 percent black succumbed to the pressure, providing only black history, black literature, black music. Only faint remonstrances on the part of black educational leaders were heard. Finally and recently the push for black English in the schools revealed the cynicism of some innovators of the educational community. Then a climax and change occurred.

Rev. Henry Nichols was the vice-president of the Board of Education. A black, he could take a forceful stand against the superintendent on this issue, showing the plan for what it was at its best: a stupid game and a backward step, keeping the black from mobility by restraining his use of the language needed for the American in urban society. Rev. Henry Nichols killed that game.

There were and still are many black educators who consider

all non-black curriculum material and culture expendable until all black children have been saturated with their own culture. But there is a growing number of blacks who urge loudly that being steeped in blackness exclusively is the path toward inequality. These men and women all over the country are warning forcefully that curriculum must prepare the black child to compete in society.

Generally teachers who ask for Motivation classes know they are undertaking a demanding assignment without being given an additional preparation period. They are aware they will be expected to do intensive work in the academic area, but they know also that they must strive to achieve the abstract goals as well: attitudinal changes, the improvement of self-concept and cultural awareness. It isn't enough for one of the Programs to stress only academic enrichment or tutoring. The cultural work, the parent participation and the community involvement are part of the student's total development.

Each teacher knows that the Program seeks out students who are considered college material but who are working below their potential. Often it takes good stretching of one's professional imagination to agree with the choices made by the coordinator and her associates. In some schools, the department heads help with the selection. In others, organization and counselors help the coordinator. But there is a wide area of criteria and some high school administrations try to broaden our target group by dropping the reading and math levels below stanine 5 to what would be roughly fifth and sixth grade when the students are entering high school. We join these administrators in their concern "for all children," but we point out that limited funds and Elementary-Secondary Education Act, Title I Guidelines dictate we must serve that group of students who will most likely succeed with the supporting services of the "M" Program in the three years of high school. No "M" school has been free of staff members who are cynical about the student selection for one reason or another. Only when the payoff comes in—of students who are successful in college, who are graduated and in professional fields—do the cynics begin to agree that they might have been wrong. But meanwhile what did their attitudes do to students? These young people felt the lack of belief in them and struggled against it, often being unable to revise their own poor self-image.

There were teachers like Mrs. Kol at West Philadelphia High School, who spent many hours a month in English class talking about her husband and sons. She resented the fact that these "mediocre" children were having their heads turned and were getting scholarships while her brilliant sons had to pay tuition. Her resentment hung chronically over the class. She ridiculed the little gold pin they wore as a reminder of their commitment. Although she had much to give them academically, her own personality problems destroyed her effectiveness with the clientele who needed her so badly. At 2:30 she cracked out of the school with military precision. Her life really began when she reached home. It took many "discussions" with the principal and department head and a few years more before she decided to go off to another school where she could find students intellectually worthier of her services.

For every example of pedestrian teaching there are many that are exciting and heartening. Florence Rose at West Philadelphia High School was an ill woman, arthritic, always in pain. But she took her role as Motivation counselor very seriously, devising ways of seeing the "M" students as often as possible. She liked children. She was holding group talks before these became fashionable. She read professional material and sought out new methods so she could give the kids the best help. Often she left the school at 5 o'clock. Often she met students and parents on Saturdays. Miss Bach, too, rarely left the counseling office before 5 o'clock, always searching for ways to help her students. Many evenings she returned to be a part of the "M" Parents meetings. Muriel Bullock was devoted to the students.

Nick Salvatore at Frankford High could have conducted his "Ethnic Backgrounds of the American People" unit with the students in their seats. But Sal took them out to visit ethnic neighborhoods, eat varied foods, hear the music and read the sociology. Then since his classroom was to be demolished and made into a corridor for the new building, he obtained permission from an extremely cooperative principal to use the walls for the painting of murals by the students. It may not have been an important work of art, but it was an important social effort to have whites, blacks and ethnic Asian students painting their human family on their wall. What happened with Sal, of course, happened to many of our coordinators and teachers. They have become so stimulated with the possibilities for intellectual growth in themselves and students that they have moved into further and deeper study of the mystery of human motivation.

Shirley Farmer, an "M" graduate who now teaches "M" English classes at Kensington High School, uses all her "M" experiences to see that the students get the same enriched program she herself received. In fact, the program she provides is more creative. It is freer—using drama, music, and the dance while her classes are learning their basic skills with their reading in psychological literature. She avails herself of all the outside talent she can find. An "M" '65 graduate who is a dancer comes to the class to demonstrate mood in dance. Another "M" '65 graduate who is now in psychology comes to lead the discussion on human behavior. Miss Farmer remembers well what motivated her and what was exciting learning. Much is being written and discussed about curriculum. In another time and place it certainly deserves many chapters. In the context of this short work I am combining the teacher with the curriculum; the material the teacher conveys becomes the frame for her attitude toward children. The youngest, least verbal student can tell you if a teacher is uninspired, unprepared, disorganized, unhappy, or dislikes the students. Their antennae are more sensitive to these classroom conditions than adults realize, and although the young people participate gleefully in some of the new, radical programs, they complain, finally, that the teachers have no teaching plan, make no demands or assignments and expect nothing of the students. "They rapped" a lot, "palled around" a lot, wore disreputable clothes and were groomed poorly. The students disdain such teachers, considering their behavior a lack of respect or regard for the students themselves.

Some wit has called these latter-day projects, "mindless programs of ecstasy." Indeed, although they seek to excite student participation, they actually produce an ill-considered dulling and an undisciplined roster of activity. What results is a smattering of inconsequential learning that has prepared the student neither for the present nor for his future. It is the teacher who must guide the student in his choices where course subjects are not designated. Even more, each teacher must examine the possibilities for development in her own curriculum.

Bess Abramovitz guided the students in BSCS, (Biological Sciences Curriculum Series), in astronomy and Heart Association-sponsored experiments. She and Elizabeth Davis believed their students could do more difficult work in biology. It was catching. Teachers listened to their associates expressing new emotions about teaching rewards and were moved to try new ideas also. The climate, which was stimulating students and parents, was motivating teachers as well. Teachers, we've said before, are human, with the same failings and the same needs as the rest of us. Teachers too must have approbation and stimulation to achieve.

I remember a student complaining, "We don't mean anything to her. She talks as if we don't have faces!" "She" was a teacher of social studies, the subject which is possibly the easiest to make relevant to our own lives. But she taught dates and events only. It was memorization from a hefty tome. If we watch the intense curiosity of children in the act of discovery, if we watch adolescents and adults as they follow with absorption a story being told, we have the model, the pattern, for what can be a successful method of teaching subject matter. In our discussion of curriculum, matter is the substance of learning and it is one with teacher and method. I have watched hungry children as they react with listlessness and apathy to learning in the class. Just so do I perceive the effect of intellectual hunger on the mind of the student. Children learn effectively from play and games. It is both independent and cooperative learning.

My friend, Betty Zlotnick, was a young reading teacher in one of Philadelphia's more difficult schools. She taught fifteen incorrigible boys of ten years old. They were always on or under the desks but never at the desks. Day after day Betty tried every technique she knew to interest the nonreading boys in books. Nothing worked.

One day, John, the leader of the group, engaged Betty in brave talk. He would get a car and take her for a ride.

"How can you get a car when you don't have a license?" Betty asked him.

"I'll get one."

"How can you get one when you can't read?"

"You mean I gotta read to get a license?"

"Yes indeed!" John was stunned into silence.

"OK!" he exploded. "What're we f----n' aroun' for. I wanna learn to read!"

Betty prepared a project. They sent for driving manuals, students drew pictures of the roadside signs they would need for a booklet. The students read, wrote, memorized, drew pictures, and bound a book. It was the busiest, proudest class on the floor. And on the last day someone stole the whole thing! But it was a motivating piece of work with many lasting rewards for all.

In the same way, the Motivation students are being guided by some of the more creative "M" teachers to learn by independent study of the humanities curriculum that I developed for the "M" Program. Given the kind of intellectual training I should like to see in our teachers, all can provide the interdisciplinary approach suggested in the curriculum. Elsewhere in this story I reported on the "Ethnic Backgrounds of the American People" unit, in which the students read sociology in *The Uprooted*, by Oscar Handlin; *Mount Allegro*, by Jerre Mangione, a story of Italian-American life; *Call It Sleep*, by Henry Roth, on Jewish immigrant life. Seven ethnic cultures were studied. Lecturers were invited to speak. Music and drama representing these cultures were brought in to class or experienced at the theater. Students sought out ethnic Americans to discuss their experiences with them. This independent study and discovery provided the students with a pleasure in learning as well as maturity and understanding.

The unit on comparative religions studied either independently or in small groups gives students the same reward. This unit is an interrelationship between religion, politics, history, painting, and music. The motivation projects provide for attendance at services of seven religious bodies. A study is made of the music and art of these religions, taking advantage of our museums and concert halls. Frances Snyder, cultural organizer at Edison High School, arranges for the class and church experiences. The parents are involved in the study and the field trips.

The humanities suggests to the "M" teachers and the students a unit on photography, in which each student works with a camera. Actually, it is a unit in sociology, for he will cover four areas of his society: (1) life with the family, (2) life with the neighbors, (3) justice and freedom, (4) politics. He will write his own script, observations, and conclusions, using questions suggested in the unit under each area of inquiry. The filming will be done as he moves about the community. Where possible, arrangements are made with the science departments for the "M" students to develop their own film in a darkroom.

Readings are suggested, as are relevant films and dramas playing in the city. This unit can be undertaken individually, although our difficult urban climate makes advisable working in small teams for safety.

Although all these humanities are interdisciplinary and cover specialty areas, no teacher need feel anxious or threatened. No teacher need be an authority in any of these subjects. Furthermore, in these days of austerity we can no longer enjoy the luxury of team teaching. Each teacher must, therefore, develop herself intellectually in all areas, preplanning and prereading.

Our students, for instance, should read *Gulliver's Travels* for the English class and hold a discussion as to its relevancy to contemporary society. Let them read Swift's observations about life in Laputa. This literature will be an amazing mirror for the student's study of our own housing administrations and their senseless destruction of hundreds of thousands of dwellings in the name of urban development.

Every "M" teacher is encouraged to involve his students in the cultural activities listed on the monthly calendar of events. The cultural events organizer works with the teachers to provide the activities. Sara Zallman, cultural organizer at South Philadelphia High School, will make all the arrangements and give orientation so that students studying sixteenth-century English history or politics will have an opportunity to integrate with their studies the film *Cromwell* and Bellini's opera *I Puritani* both on stage and in recording. The use of Sir Kenneth Clark's *Civilisation* series provides a rich resource for the study of the humanities in the "M" class joined with involvement in the city's cultural life.

With the exception of Betty Zlotnick's reading class, the Motivation models have centered on high-school-level, college-bound "M" students. Similar techniques scaled down or changed in varied ways can be motivational for all ages.

Last year, anticipating the advent of the Salzburg Marionettes performing *Snow White*, I prepared a project for a class of severely deprived, undereducated, inner-city fourth-graders. These were non-readers, and quite impoverished children. With the help of a special Fels Foundation grant and a dedicated teacher, Jacqui Gordon, a program was set up.

Each student had his own *Classic Comics* copy of "Snow White." The students read the book in class and at home. At the end of two weeks the class and several parents attended the marionette performance by the famous troupe. In the ensuing days, the students discussed the experience, taping their class discussions on a cassette recorder. Then they wrote a letter to the donor of the grant. Finally, they undertook in small groups the writing of short, original playlets and performed these with marionettes of their own making.

The principal, teacher, and parents were very enthusiastic about the new excitement they saw in this class for the first time and were impressed with the variety of skills the children were learning in the spirit of fun.

Within a few weeks I shall undertake a motivational project with secondary-school mentally retarded students. The teacher will read the *Fiddler on the Roof* while the music will be playing in their classroom. After the students have mastered the reading, the class and teacher will attend a showing of the film. Verbal skills will be stressed after the film is seen.

As the suggestions in the foregoing pages are read, many will say: "Of course, it's beautiful! But try it without money!" And they're right. If these games, activities, and curriculum innovations are worthwhile and if we mean business for our children, the money must be found.

Very little can be initiated and accomplished without funds. Teachers have to live with our inflated economy, cultural establishments must "make it" financially—although all (with the exception of some theater moguls) have seen fit to give us huge discounts. They agree with me that only in this way will their ends be served—that is, the creation of future audiences. Often in promoting the Program, the students and goals, I tell businessmen that the economics indicate that college graduates are responsible for greater purchasing power, real estate, travel, clothing, culture, etc. Notwithstanding the fake tales of a glut of college graduates, we'd better improve our economic system so that a man with a college degree can hold his rightful place in society. Thus, Dr. Clark Kerr, in his report sponsored by the Carnegie Commission on Higher Education, wrote: "Going to college—any college—does give to the individual a chance for a more satisfying life and to society the likelihood of a more effective community." This, after all, is our goal in the "M" Program.

I should like to make a few comments about early childhood motivation, since this chapter has been concerned with some non-secondary school experiences.

For three decades I have fought a lonely battle to start the education of the child almost immediately after birth. In my layman's concept (physiologically and metaphorically) I saw the brain as a fairly unprogrammed instrument onto which early impressions were imprinted to make the person what he became. Therefore, I felt the parent should start as soon as possible to provide pleasurable learning stimuli to the infant. I met with fierce antagonism even up until eight years ago from people who resisted "intellectualizing," "pushing," children too early. Let's dispose of the word "pushing," for all of us resist any activity into which we are pushed. I believe that from earliest infancy a child's intellect should be expanded, exposed to various stimuli. This has been encouraged in this decade with the availability of playpen and crib mobiles and thousands of other "educational toys."

In the Jewish family of the small shtetl of Eastern Europe, learning held such high priority that it was traditional to put a few drops of honey on a siddur, a holy book, and to allow a small child to lick the honey. In this way he was to "absorb" the love of a book and learning.

Every smell, color, texture, and movement is a new, imprinted experience that is meaningful to the child's cultural development. It doesn't mean that expensive educational toys are the only way to give the baby the stimuli. Every home has hundreds of such "educational toys" used by the parents in the course of the day. It's nice, but not necessary, to be able to buy a child's xylophone. As a substitute, I was able to find six pot lids with different tones and fine timbre. These have withstood abuse by my vigorous children and their children. The important thing here is to provide the child with the mind stretchers, the experiences that will draw him from exposure to pleasure and from interest to interest.

"He'll learn all these things in due time," or, "He'll get it all when he starts school." I think that's too late. Children should have accumulated a good deal of their culture before grade one. Exposure to zoos, to museums, pushing buttons to see the relationship between one's finger's pressure and the activation of a train, or lights, are experiences that will stimulate the child's creative and intellectual development. By the time the child has entered school he will have banked the widest spectrum of motivating stimuli. This storage doesn't ensure permanent motivation all through life, but it can give the person a wide sphere of interests, which will help his self-esteem, and which will prevent the deadly lassitude that comes of intellectual boredom. Much of this is a result of devastating boredom with life and its sameness, even into adulthood.

In discussions with Motivation Parents during their monthly meetings, I encouraged them to undertake with their younger children the kinds of activities the "M" students were having, and it gave me much pleasure to learn that the younger siblings called themselves "M" kids and wanted to go and do and experience.

The Government is on the threshold of undertaking a vast network of day-care centers. I hope it will take the initiative in ensuring that these will be educational and developmental centers rather than custodial ingatherings. I feel, too, that we must undertake massive programs of early diagnosis of neurological damage, which produces a wide spectrum of learning disabilities and handicaps. Many of these are easily correctable at an early age, and much can be accomplished nutritionally and educationally by parents. With these newer concepts and programs we may perhaps anticipate that students of the future will have fewer motivational problems.

A new direction for the Motivation Program—
Bartram Motivation School

11

Groton-On-The-Dumps

Dr. Joseph N. Brancato, vice-principal of South Philadelphia High School, has said of the Motivation Program, "It is one of the few programs sponsored by the School District of Philadelphia which has gained recognition from educators outside our city; but more important, it has proven itself through results which have been documented."

Where are we going with a program that has served over four thousand "M" graduates, of whom over three quarters have been through college and are in business and professional life? Dr. Sidney Marland's HEW report confirms what we discovered in nine years of the Motivation Program's operation: that this type of supporting help, academic and cultural, is needed by all children, even those of "superior" intellect. Only thus can successful progress toward higher education be achieved and sustained.

Should we continue in the same direction with the same methods? Are the conditions within and outside the schools the same as those that spurred the birth of the Program? Are the needs and physical situations different?

Everything is the same in these ten years and yet nothing is the same. We still have hundreds of thousands of students who will never live up to their potential and we will all be the poorer for it. The tendency to depreciate other humans is still rife among those who've "made it." We need greater numbers of trained leaders and yet some voices decry sending to college "so many who don't belong there." They say: "We will need fewer college-trained people. We have a glut." Then there are cynical people in each school who deplore giving so much to the four hundred Motivation students when the money should be spread evenly over the school to four thousand. And even as a few weak administrators advance this self-serving criticism, they are watering down the Program that has brought success to so many.

It is easy to break down a well-structured machine but it is infinitely more difficult to build one up. Essentially what is required for the effort to build is the need and the will. The need and the will were responsible for the establishment of the Bartram High Motivation School in September, 1971. Just so was West Philadelphia High's Motivation Program born in 1962; the need and the will were there.

Bartram stands physically and socially in a confluence of problems. Once a respected academic school with an Italian-Jewish population, the student composition is now black-Italian. The school had four thousand students, more than it could house. To accommodate them, the school went on a morning and afternoon shift. The educational program immediately became a victim of this compromise.

Whoever was at fault is not the subject of this chapter, but student race-warfare erupted in the school and the neighborhood, and this precipitated the changes out of which came our Motivation School.

Elsewhere I have written that this was an early dream that I had formulated but that had faded immediately; its time had not yet come. Now the need and the will made the dream a reality. The community insisted that tensions would be eased by reducing school population. It urged that groups of students be sent to other schools. At this point I resurrected my old dream, and it was accepted as a feasible plan. Briefly, the "M" Program, as it was being conducted at Bartram, was lifted bodily with its 350 students of tenth, eleventh, and twelfth grades. They were transported with twelve teachers of English, math, social studies, language, science, and typing, and with a counselor, two secretaries, a cultural organizer, and a coordinator to a little red brick schoolhouse of 1905 vintage.

The Bartram Motivation School, Groton-On-The-Dumps, stands on the smoking dunes and close by Philadelphia International Airport, on lonely, vacant farmland surrounded by marshes and the huge tanks belonging to Gulf Oil. During the warm months of September and October the students suffered attacks of gnats and fleas, which came out of the vegetation. Field mice came in to enjoy the humanity. During the two months of icy cold, the freezing air whistled through the old window frames; water entered through the roof's fissures. Generally, the physical setup might have been fine for an elementary school fifty years ago, but it is inadequate as an academic high school in 1972.

Despite all the shortcomings—the heat, the cold, the insects, the distance from home, and the long bus ride—there is a minimum of absenteeism. Only illness keeps the kids home. There is no cutting. The penalty might be separation from the Program. Of the twelve teachers, four had been loathe to come out to the marshes. They came only because reduction in staff at the home school made it an either-or for them. Now in time for September, 1972, we are told there will be grievances filed by the teachers union unless others have the opportunity to go to the "M" school. At the same time the Bartram "M" teachers voice what fifty Motivation teachers around the city say: "The Program does something to the kids and to us. It makes us like one another, and there's learning going on."

It's a "swinging" school in every way, with a beautiful young coordinator, Dena Obus, who plans, demands, cajoles, and achieves. She has high expectations and sees to it that the students are getting a thorough academic preparation. It is tied up with that overused but healthy word "relevance." The school is moving toward an interdisciplinary approach. Formal classwork takes place in four days. The fifth is left for tutoring, for teacher-student conferences, for staff development conferences or for unusual events such as concerts or lectures or trips to colleges and trips to other cities to experience their cultural institutions. An open *Friday Seminar Day* will provide a choice of activities for sophomores, juniors, and seniors for two-hour time spans. The tenth-year students may take a workshop on the preparation of performance, which will be demonstrated by a city theater group. The visiting troupe demonstrates the techniques for portraying tragedy, comedy, and farce, explaining what is needed in the writing to project these drama forms. They invite the students to participate as demonstrators.

Another group of students may select a chamber music workshop with Norman Johns, cellist ("M" '68), and Charles Pettiway, pianist. Each musician will play representative music of several musical eras, demonstrating the use of the instrument by the composers. After the recital, there will be an open discussion in which students will become familiar with the possibilities of portraying human emotions (sorrow, anger, humor, satire, disdain) on the musical instruments.

A group may desire to engage in psychodrama, in musical composing, choir, dance, folk music.

Since the school is close to the Tinicum Wildlife Preserve, a group of interested bird watchers will be free to pursue this experience.

Those interested in sports can find the games in the yard and grounds around the school. For the more extensive sports like football, the students go back to the home school, a few miles away. Indoor games like chess, scrabble, and bridge are available.

And finally, for a given Friday there will be a roster of lecturers on various topics—a radio personality or the director of a radio or television station; an assistant district attorney to discuss community problems; an ornithologist; a biologist, a lecturer on ecology using the nearby Delaware River, the airport, the swamps, and the Wildlife Preserve as the laboratory. Jack Bookbinder, renowned artist and Director of Art Education for the city's schools, will lecture on "Art and the Humanities" with film and music demonstrating selected art periods. The important aspect of the lecture is the students' association with this wonderful man. This is a sampling of a Friday roster of events that the Bartram "M" students may select.

Teachers are actively involved in the development of their curriculum and programs. Expecting that the site would be selected for the national bicentennial exposition, one social studies teacher developed a citizen-interest project, having his "M" students survey the widespread neighboring community for reactions to the 1976 fete. It was an exercise in citizenship, history, economics, housing, and human concern.

An English teacher who has musical experience has guided her group in the writing of a musical, and the group will perform this work at the time of "M" graduation. A history and an English teacher are combining their two disciplines in a large study unit with joint discussion, with trips to the public library for term paper preparation.

The school is free in spirit, yet structured. Although there are bells and seating is in classrooms rather than in halls or on floors, students feel a more relaxed atmosphere. Even as they are constrained by rules, they grant that the rules are necessary if all the kids are to have the same number and quality of privileges. Mainly they express pleasure in the easy relationship they have with their teachers and in the fact that they feel everyone in the program is interested in the welfare of each student and the quality of education the kids are getting. This, after all, is the focus of each of the "M" Programs.

We have in this school what we should like to have in our other Programs—that is, a counselor who will work exclusively with this "M" group of three hundred to five hundred students from tenth through twelfth grade. Bartram Motivation is fortunate in having Dr. Jeanette Pontz, who is a friend, counselor, guide, and, simply, a person kids love to drop in on, if only for a word. "Did you go to hear P. D. Q. Bach yesterday! Great!" Even those "M" students who are traditionally nondisruptive will be assured of this counselor's time for their problems. This is not so, often in a few of the other Programs.

Our psychologists, Dr. Sara Taubin and Thomas Pierce, have held Open Talk Groups with students and parents. In this school we shall start the Open Talk Sessions for parents, alone, to help them learn the secrets of communication with their children. This is a new technique, undertaken to find another avenue that will give students greater mobility, and peace with the family.

There are no drugs on the scene, but we are aware and want to provide the support the students need to help them withstand pressures from this sinister invasion.

The atmosphere, the proprietary feelings, are rather obvious to all visitors. The kids are proud of their prep school and want to handle their peer problems themselves whenever possible.

Graffiti is a no-no in their freshly painted old barn of a school. It happened once in a hall. Just a five-inch black initial. The artist evidently felt the anger of the student body, because no more of his art appeared.

But there was one other serious incident, which occurred right after the second report card came out. Someone had shown anger by rifling desks, writing on walls in the classrooms, and stealing the roll books. The teachers were unhappy. The students were angry and the atmosphere became tense.

In somewhat the same style as had been used by "M" '66 at West Philadelphia High, years before, a self-appointed group of three students decided to find the culprit. After much quiet questioning, they found the guilty student—one of their peers, not an infiltrator as had been thought. They assembled the teachers involved and told them the guilty one had been found; that he was distraught knowing his identification would mean removal from the school.

The committee said the student offered full reparation—a return of the money, the roll books, and a paint job to cleanse the walls if the teachers would agree not to punish him more drastically. An agreement was made. The young man has fulfilled his part of the bargain.

In all activities and problems the student body is exhibiting responsibility and an acceptance of a "motivation code of behavior" which all the Programs seem to achieve.

Hoping to avoid traditional means of punishment for lateness, one of the teachers organized a talk group to deal with it. In the discussion, students realized their lateness was harming their grades. Thus, they had a constructive reason to change the pattern. They made various "confessions," each explaining his chronic lateness to the group. Then they discussed in pairs. Each took a turn explaining while the other acted as the counselor, giving an honest criticism of the excuse. Each student slowly realized that all excuses were just that. They could get to school on time despite "infrequent bus runs," "mother wasn't well," "couldn't find a blouse," etc.

With this discussion technique, some have shown marked improvement and the groups will be continued. This technique is useful also in some of our Programs where conflict has arisen around a particular teacher. If this talk group is activated before a serious eruption takes place, with the coordinator available for the "balancing," much grief can be avoided.

The cultural activities are integral to the curriculum and are a built-in element of it. Gloria Moskowitz, the cultural organizer, who can get blood from a stone, can also get the most esoteric concert to sound like a jam session. At least she gets the students to try varied styles of art. "You don't have to take a season ticket! Just try one sample!" In this school, teachers and students go together to a multitude of events, taking on "culture" as their rightful heritage. It's paid off for many. They've come to enjoy such things.

Gloria seeks out hosts for their Host Visits who will provide the students with what they need: intellectual stimulation, fun, pride in race, pride in one's own ability to rap about many topics, ease with people who are different from oneself. An evening

Groton-On-The-Dumps

with Hugh Masakela, after his trumpet concert, was very rewarding to the young men and women of Bartram Motivation. He discussed his music with them. He let them talk about their lives here, then drew them into a comparison with his life in South Africa. "Life is much better here. Here a black man can do anything. In South Africa a black cannot move without a pass." The youth didn't let his thinking pass unchallenged. They argued with him, but they were impressed with the fact that he could not go home lest he lose his life or freedom.

Another evening Dr. Chaim Potok and his wife, Dena, were hosts to a group. The "M" students read *The Chosen* in advance and thus were able to engage in a full intellectual discussion with Dr. Potok analyzing characters, their motivation, history, and religion.

The wealth that exists in the community to serve students as hosts is tremendous. A Host Visit with Yitzhak and Susan Sankowsky cannot be measured in terms of what a student has come away with. Yitzhak is a celebrated painter who talks art with the young people; it always comes out as humanism, which is what the Sankowsky art is all about. Susan is a social studies department head at Bartram High School and an author of consequence. Together, integrating their artistic fields, they are a formidable pair of hosts. The evening is a highly satisfactory and pleasant one for the young guests. The spillover into the next day's classes is a by-product from which many more of the "M" students will gain. In all of the "M" Programs, the Host Visit is a highly productive project.

The monthly evening meeting of the "M" Parents Group jams the cafeteria as if free prizes were being given out. A father told his employer, who told me, that they'd put five children through school but had never before experienced a child being unwilling to stay home with a sore throat. He'd never seen so many fathers and mothers appear every month just to show support for the Motivation School. Bus drivers say they haven't seen kids like these in a long time—no graffiti, no ripped seats; courtesy, respect, and fun on all the trips.

But all is not yet undiluted joy. Many promises were made by the School District in an effort to open the school after only six weeks of preparation. Little was ready. Our college-bound students have an inadequate science laboratory and equipment. There is no library whatsoever; nor is there a public library within three miles of the school. There is no physical education equipment or audio-visual equipment.

Yet, there is no hostility; there is some resentment that promises were not kept, but no anger. They raise their voices to request and demand but not with violence. It is their school, a private school in the best tradition with the features stressed in the Title I guidelines of parent and student participation. It is their facility, albeit a decrepit one, a model of what our society will have to undertake in the future: smaller school units serving smaller groups of children. Apartment complexes will do well to plan the school area within their context. Business centers, shopping areas close to children's homes, will have to combine enclaves for public schooling. There will be temporary shortcomings in these new schools, but the salutary effects on students and community of these extended living, working, and learning facilities will be permanent.

Finally, Groton-On-The-Dumps is really an expression of the middle-class aspirations of most of our students and their parents. They want all the advantages and goodies they've been reading about in literature describing middle- and upper-income Americans. It is the students who bring to school the ideas for the various experiences. Despite its climate as a private school, Bartram Motivation is a public school designed to serve a homogeneous group of young citizens of varied ethnic backgrounds, who will absorb their intellectual and cultural development with pleasure while they are developing for their own fulfillment and for service to our society.

After Thoughts

In the preceding chapters I have moved in and out of an eleven-year time span attempting to describe the social and educational climate at a given moment in the development of the Motivation Program. Projects undertaken in the early '60s had to prove themselves in what they were meant to do for the "M" students. Proof meant results for children. If there wasn't enough payoff, the project was either dropped or revised. At West High, the original school, Henry Weisberg, our English head, amended, enriched and cut out. Nothing in the curriculum was sacred. Isadore Klingsberg continually engaged his math staff in efforts to discover new ways of stimulating kids, implanting math concepts and skills. In the 1971 "M" Seminar, he provided the leadership to project further the possibilities for new, motivational math programs.

By July, 1966, there were enough tangible results to give the Program permanent status. It was no longer an experiment. It was a stable inner current in the large stream of the school. The 1965 "M" class had sixty-four students accepted to college. June, 1966, saw eighty-one going into college. Approximately 75 percent of each "M" group were matriculating and were staying in. The evaluation of 1969 showed 81 percent going through the second year in the face of appalling national attrition figures in the first year of college.

There were many intangibles. There were two dropouts in the two groups of 265 students. The cutting of class was negligible and frowned upon by the "M" students themselves. They were accepting intellectual and social standards that had been foreign to the school for at least seven or eight years, predating the impassioned scolding by E. Washington Rhodes in 1961.

More important, the "M" students had become a cadre of responsible young leaders who had no doubt where they wanted to go.

These results were glamorous enough to persuade the program planners of the School District of Philadelphia, prodded by School Board member George Hutt, to make the Motivation Program available to five thousand "non-star" students of Philadelphia's urban schools. Using the same model and the same goals, fifteen inner-city schools accepted the program. Twelve were to receive funds through Title I. The other three did not qualify, technically, for poverty funds, although the student populations of these schools had changed greatly in the last few years and many were poverty students. These three schools received School District funds. Within a half year of the establishment of the Program in the fifteen schools, Title I funds were cut. Immediately this meant the removal of the special counselor. The next year the funds were cut further. This meant that the Program lost one of the three added teachers. Other services were cut out. By 1970 the School District faced financial disaster and the "M" Programs funded by the District were cut drastically. Highly productive "M" Programs at these three schools were reduced to a skeleton project unworthy of the name or money. Despite the Title I slashes those Programs survived and, in several schools, flourished. When this occurred it was a result of the principal's, coordinator's, students', teachers', and parents' determination.

We had an early sample of what responsible student power could accomplish when, in 1968, we faced the withdrawal of Title I funds and the demise of the Motivation Program. Two "M" students from Overbrook High School's Program, Ruthie

Fogel and Ronald Felton, organized a protest committee composed of students and parents of fifteen schools. They came to the School Board meeting held in the administration building, several picketing with their signs, others being given the opportunity to speak to the Board in its public meeting. They spoke so responsibly and effectively that William Ross, a Board member, urged the Board to instruct its federal programs director that the Motivation Program should receive priority if it prepared students so impressively. The students' performance before the Board was in sharp contrast to the violence and obscene verbal abuse hurled at the Board several weeks before. The point was that the "M" students had been convinced it was their Program, it was serving them well, and that as citizens they could plead for their best interest, but responsibly, not with violent confrontation. They and their parents had believed me, and through me their coordinators, when we urged them to accept responsibility for their education, telling them that the schools were theirs and they had to let us know how they wanted to be educated. We felt we were educating our "M" students for future leadership of our community not in violence but in rational citizenship, not in sit-ins, in taking over the school auditorium, not in bursting into the principal's office whenever it pleased some disgruntled students to do so. We agreed that three hundred years of waiting was enough but insisted they'd have to get their rights without destroying anyone else's in the process.

It was a difficult time. While we were urging peaceful and reasonable action, another department of the School District was urging the students into confrontation. As this professional leadership itself bragged, "We introduced the students and community to strategies." At another time they said, "Some people saw our work as plotting with the students." The same leadership introduced what was termed "guerrilla theatre" in an effort to "sensitize" the white administrators.

During a meeting of top administrators at Fellowship House, ironically, a group of blacks burst into the room firing guns, screaming, running around threateningly. In terror, many of the men and women dropped to the floor. Only a few remained standing and observing. They were ready to assist the paid actors, who were actually gang members, should the administrators seek to defend themselves against the "criminals." These were top officials who had staged this violent confrontation to help whites understand the tensions and frustrations of the ghetto dwellers.

There were people in that room with heart trouble, whose contribution to the children of the city covered two or three decades. When the guerrilla theatre was explained to them there was disgust, fear, anger, and general disenchantment with the top leadership for having initiated and permitted this irresponsible and dangerous action. As for me, I was frightened that ostensibly enlightened, concerned School District leadership had become so enmeshed in the excitement of confrontation that they could conceive of it as education for leadership and politics.

The Motivation Program of which I have spoken in these pages is really a minute project in the context of a huge, complicated educational structure. It serves five thousand although it should serve 284 thousand. Its visible goal is the student's acceptance into and his stability in college. I have lived with the program these ten years; I have retained my friendship with former "M" students, graduates from high school and college, and soon from professional schools; I continue to see their parents. "M" grads have become a kind of fraternity around the city. They don't wear the gold pin but they acknowledge with pride the designation it had given them as "M" students.

It happens almost every day that a phone call elicits from the other end, "Mrs. Segal! This is Jerome Roy, "M" '67!" My frequent visits to the schools give me continued and refreshing reminders, as I find our "M" grads in front of the classrooms, that most of these young people "should never have gone to college." At least that's what the doubters had warned me.

After Thoughts

"Don't encourage them in what they cannot achieve." And yet they achieved—even those who didn't go on to college immediately. They worked a year, or went to war. Tom Dorsey, for example, has used his academic training to move upward in the most technical aspects of the Air Force. But the new idea of themselves was planted deeply and needed only the rearrangement of life's difficult pieces to begin functioning.

This is a small program but it is a tremendous one in terms of what it says about people. In this case the people are the young, the defenseless and impressionable. It says we'd better take a look at what our attitudes are toward our children, tomorrow's citizens.

I read that we are a child-oriented society. Not only is this pompous professionalese; it is also untrue. For ours is a culture of silent violence toward our young; a culture that tolerates the highest infant motality rate of the free world. We permit children's undernourishment to the point of mental deterioration. We allow them to be born into a world poisoned with lead, DDT and nuclear fallout. In Philadelphia we provide about $900 a year to undereducate a schoolchild to lead the good life, but nationally we are willing to spend $7500 to educate an eighteen-year-old soldier to kill another. The 1972 figures show that seven cents of every dollar in the national budget goes to education; seventy-seven cents goes to defense. Ours is a society that permits sick parents to batter their children with virtual impunity. Ours is a democracy in which a juvenile has fewer rights in the court than does a vicious adult offender.

No, we are not a child-oriented society, nor an adult one. We are a culture organized to achieve immediate gratification, gained with our economic power. In the nation's drive for this power the individual has always been of the least importance, whether it was the black slave in the field, the Italian immigrant laying the railroad bed, or the Jew slaving in the sweatshop. The name of the game was the dollar, not the man. Even today the improvement of the quality of life is possible, but our national leadership lacks the same will to achieve as do our students.

I said a few pages ago that the invisible, intangible goal is the development of one's self-love, one's appreciation of his God-given potential for human endeavor. The college goal and the academic program needed to get there was a vehicle for his dignity and self-enrichment so that his life, and the lives he would touch generations hence, will have achieved an enduring meaning. The "M" Program showed how a small segment in the total school program could be made to serve children because of what it did to the child's spirit and to the hopes of his parents. The same high goals can be achieved by millions of children whose career goals may be other than college; children with simple or severe learning disabilities; those, indeed, who have sustained brain damage.

We are embarking on a vocational education "kick" in this decade, being as we are, a faddist society. With all that needs doing in "thinking out" the improvement to our planet's condition, we decide now that too many are going to college. We need more skilled laborers; and we do. But will the skilled craftsman or laborer of the future be willing to be a slave to the machine or the job? Forty years ago Charles Chaplin, in his film *Modern Times,* portrayed the dehumanization of the man on the assembly line. We have not yet begun to assess what happens to a man who does nothing other than turn bolts on a wheel all day. In 1972, the greatest business brains in the world still refuse to understand the significance of crippling absenteeism among workers; nor are they reading the loud, clear signals of the gigantic amount of human error, which is, in the end, costly not only to industry but to life itself. I see these signs as a rebellion of the human spirit, which is as much a revolution as the earliest tragic union battles for human dignity and decent working conditions.

If my analysis is correct, what then should the educational establishment be doing to prepare the children for a new kind of future? Each child must be given an academic program while he is being exposed to many vocational arts. He may not wish to spend his life as a skilled craftsman but he will have the pleasure of performing with his hands for his own familial needs. At the same time he will accept the dignity and the needs of professional craftsmen.

As for the vast army of men and women who are our skilled artisans, they too must be prepared with a knowledge and appreciation of our multi-faceted cutural heritage. They will not be willing much longer to be an unreasoning part of the machine, but will want to be part of the leisure life that must come inevitably. They are telling us clearly as did W. E. B. Du Bois that "the purpose of education is not to make a man an artisan, but to make an artisan a man."

If the "child is father of the man," we will perforce have to start early in his childhood to let him know what he means to himself and to us as a nation. We will have to implant in him the knowledge that in his manhood he will have to take the direction in promoting our democratic society. We must teach him in every program of the school that we care deeply for him, that his goals and ours are indivisible.

This we must do in every classroom, in every school of the nation, with honesty and integrity, for this child is the center of our world. In all of our behavior as a nation we must let him know that he is wanted and needed by his fellowmen. If we mean this, we will then prepare a nation and an environment in which he can thrive, in which he will know hope.

Appendix

In connection with my present responsibility as Specialist for Motivational Programs with the School District of Philadelphia, I asked friends, associates and observers of the Motivation Program if they would hold a "conversation" with me about the Program. I sent them a form with questions such as:

(1) Was this Program more believable than some others with which you've been associated? Why?

(2) Why were the "M" parents more involved and interested than are the parents of the general school population?

(3) Some educators and psychologists are ready to write off high school students as being too old to have their patterns changed. Your work with the Program would show you didn't agree with this concept. Will you develop your thinking?

(4) As parent or student when did you begin to see change?

(5) Commissioner of Education Sidney Marland's report states that "contrary to general thinking, students who believe they will go to college, do not do so unless encouraged by special programs," such as the Motivation Program. Will you respond to this statement with your experience in the Program.

Some of the many respondents used my question form for their answers. Others preferred to write beyond the simple scope of the form. I believe the responses make a revealing statement. With almost no exception the respondents have agreed with our view of the principles governing human motivation, what people are capable of, and what the "M" Program proved. The responses that follow then can be a dramatically condensed guide for motivation.

THE SUPERIOR COURT OF PENNSYLVANIA
JUDGE'S CHAMBERS
364 CITY HALL
PHILADELPHIA 19107

March 8, 1972

Mrs. Rebecca Segal
Specialist for Motivational Programs
School District of Philadelphia

Dear Rebecca:

It will be my pleasure to talk to you about the Program.

I immediately became interested in the Motivation Program because I thought it was one of the few logical, pragmatic, intelligent and sensible approaches to one of the most difficult sociological problems of our day.

I observed that the principles of the Program were faithfully executed and that the children dramatically changed and I was tremendously encouraged to see how many children were being guided toward positive and productive goals. It is the antithesis of the hopeless scenes I witnessed thousands of times in Juvenile Court.

APPENDIX

One of the most gratifying aspects of the Motivation Program was to see the many Motivation Parents who turned out month after month each time I visited with them. The parents recognized the deep concern, solicitude, sympathy and understanding that was projected by this Program and they responded.

Unfortunately, many youngsters from underprivileged homes or who are poorly motivated or both do not have the self-esteem nor the desire to think in terms of college. I fully subscribe to the belief that incentive programs such as Motivation give the necessary impetus to those students who by reason of their background, experience, ineptitude or misdirection were floundering.

The Program is especially important in light of the new findings by behaviorists and biologists.

For years educators and others believed that learning patterns were fixed early in life and were unalterable. This is palpably absurd. In my own experience I have seen literally hundreds of young people who were apparently doomed to a disastrous existence ignited by a spark which catapulted them into a new, meaningful and productive life.

My wife and I considered it a privilege to be associated with the Program as Hosts and with Parents because we believed this Program treated children with dignity, titillated their curiosity, inspired them to accomplishments and encouraged them to attain goals.

Best wishes.

                Cordially,

                J. SYDNEY HOFFMAN
                Judge

February 4, 1972

Dear Mrs. Segal:

I want to reconstruct some of my memories and my feelings about our Program.

The Motivation Program (concentrated as it was at that time) in West Philadelphia High School was reaching out to the Sulzberger Junior High School where my daughter was a student. As it was explained to me the program sought to stimulate excellent achievement in academic studies. At that time—the early sixties—there was little stimulus being offered the children in the schools. (Of course there was always the master teacher here and there who challenged young minds.) The Motivation Program then seemed a whole new emphasis on excellence in academic studies with a structure which included extra classes in these subjects, opportunities to explore with practitioners chosen fields of endeavor. With such tangible and practical steps a part of the Motivation Program it seemed that there was real and serious intent to improve the education process.

The Motivation Parents became more involved and interested because the Motivation Program was involved and interested in their children. Thru the Motivation Program their child became known to his teachers, heads of departments, and counselors: he came to know them as people who expected the best from him. In achievement, aspirations, goals and conduct only the best was acceptable from him. For some parents this was reinforcement and support of their own aspirations and expectations for their children. To some others, the Motivation Program gave them a new look at their child and a new evaluation of his potential.

The major factor in making this Motivation Program the most promising and hopeful program to date is the determination of the director, coupled with dogged persistence, to involve the parents in

APPENDIX

the planning, goals, and implementation of the various special projects which were a part of the Motivation Program. The extra classes in mathematics, science and literature recommended and explained by the director required the parents' support and cooperation. Secondly, and equally significant to the success of the program was the one-to-one counseling given to children and parents as part of the program—in studies and in personal adjustment.

My interest in the Motivation Program was stimulated by the major goal of the program—that of getting the potential college student into some college. Familiar as I am with the high school student who should be college-bound, but who because he is achieving below his potential or the home situation provides no motivation is "just passing," I am well aware of this valuable human resource which could be saved and directed into a responsible or leadership role in our cities. This the Motivation Program had set out to do.

Mrs. Segal, In response to your question about changing patterns. If there are psychologists and educators who feel that high school students are too old to have their patterns changed, this is regrettable. One of the main ingredients in the level of achievement is the concept of self-worth and self-image. The regard in which a human being is held by his fellows, his family, his teachers, can affect his valuation of self. No honest person will say that a youngster in his teens cannot and will not be affected by being convinced of a greater ability than he has demonstrated. It is a human trait to respond to a favorable estimate of oneself and when this is reinforced by test results, teacher expectation and family support, achievement improves. Studies have reported that the teacher expectation factor alone has brought about upgrading by 2 or 3 points in student performance. This can work adversely also.

In my own child the Motivation Program was the perfect climate and perfect association. She had only one standard—excellence. She grew in self-criticism and in self-confidence. For many children whom I came to know, the potential being there, the growth in self-confidence, competitiveness and a beginning clarification in personal goals became apparent. The challenge and support of the expanded academic program brought a brighter gleam to the eyes of these students for academic achievement than had heretofore been apparent. This began to manifest itself at different stages with each child. Here the involvement of the parent (family), one of the basics of the Motivation Program, was definitely a critical factor. For some, this change came in the 10th grade, for some later; but whenever, this significant change did take place.

Better than some, I can respond to the Commissioner of Education's report on college-bound students and the factor of encouragement. Regrettably, many who have the potential are lost to us via the "just passing" performance, graduation from high school with no further goal in education, to jobs which demand little of them and most regrettably the drop-out route. Were these youngsters picked up at age 13 or 14 by a Motivation Program such as we have in Philadelphia, we would not have this waste of our most important human resource. Students and parents in the Motivation are made to see that the student is society's investment in the future. They are the most precious resource mankind has and one which can grow in value the more it is used, watered in the academic curriculum, sunned in the encouragement and challenges of the master teacher and counselor to blossom, even in stony ground, to light up the world of education, science, medicine, business, the humanities.

Unquestionably the Motivation Program has secured for us some of the most promising workers in society's vineyard. It is a safeguard against waste of human resources and a strengthening of an ordered society.

>Sincerely yours,
>
>CATHERINE S. MCCABE
>Parent, "M" '67

APPENDIX

THE SCHOOL DISTRICT OF PHILADELPHIA
BOARD OF EDUCATION
PARKWAY AT TWENTY-FIRST STREET

February 7, 1972

MEMO TO: Mrs. Rebecca Segal
Specialist, Motivational Programs

FROM: George Hutt

1. One of the tragedies of large school systems is that one tends to rationalize failures instead of building on success. In spite of large failures small successes do exist and I sensed that the program at West Philadelphia would be worthwhile looking into as a proof that the job *can be done* for young people and that they and the parents will respond under proper conditions.

2. This program was more believable than any other program because the results were more observable. Most programs are "written up" in a blanket of pedagogical and academic terms which one can take or leave based on their own inclination. "The results of this program and its believability were based on actual achievements in terms of the success stories of the students involved."

3. This program has been more promising than others because one way to measure a program is in terms of an input–output relationship which defines efficiency. This is not a gimmick program, but one based on achievement and success through coming to grips with unmet needs in the educational program. Its effect was sound from a human as well as an academic point of view.

4. The motivation parents were more interested and involved than parents of the general school population because they too shared in

the "halo" effect as a consequence of their children developing a sense of self worth and dignity. This reflected back to the parents who as parents of the children also developed new values and prospectives as a result of their involvement. The tandem effect took place.

5. I am not sure that psychologists can be considered educators, but it is true that both are ready to write off high school students as being too old to have their patterns changed. I think this kind of thinking marks the differences between social scientists and physical scientists. Physical scientists operate in a realm where things are possible, the only difficulties being that some things are much more difficult than others. I would never agree that any person or situation is beyond improvement, it is just harder in some cases than others. The "faint of heart" are prone to classify difficult jobs or things that they have failed to do as impossibilities. Consequently, we need little success stories to show them that they are wrong and "copping out."

GEORGE HUTT
Member, Board of Education

COLLEGE OF HOME ECONOMICS
DREXEL UNIVERSITY
PHILADELPHIA 19104

March 1, 1972

Dear Rebecca:

The "M" students who attend my Open Talk Groups think of themselves as "second best." They start with a low opinion of themselves and their peers. They are concerned about whether they are normal adolescents. But the fact that they are selected for special goals, that we think they are fine, that we heed their advice and experience, the fact that the Program has stability and prestige in the school and that with its continuity their younger sisters and brothers will be in it, make it a sound and permanent educational experience.

I see and hear in the group many unhappy but normal parent–student conflicts. But at least the certainty for the future, of one's ability to have some of the action has been solidified by the Program. I see them and their parents putting aside the vague plans and dreams and stating unequivocally high aspirations they wish to achieve.

In addition to validating the essential normality, competence and decency of these families we go one step further. We teach and practice simple principles of good human interraction. That is, the students are helped to understand some of their typical ways of handling situations and people. We help them to examine their methods to see if they can achieve their own goals in this way. We reiterate the goals, namely academic achievement, getting on with peers, teachers and parents. When they find that their techniques are self-defeating, we develop with them simple and functional behavior changes.

Every technique and the goals are intended to give students the ability to use judgment and responsibility in their daily lives. Best,

        Cordially,

        DR. SARA TAUBIN
        Psychologist with the Program
           since 1965

January 24, 1972

Dear Rebecca:

The goals of the Motivation Program as we originally defined them so many years ago, were limited, clear and attainable; progress was statistically measurable. I noticed great changes in the direction of college orientation within the school population. In later years, when the goals were made less clear (at West) and when the Program enjoyed less inspired leadership and administrative support, the Program faltered. Thus fewer children achieved the goals of the Program and developed as we knew they could.

You ask about the desirability of involving the entire school rather than a concentrated group in this Program. It does not seem logical; on the contrary, to scattershot limited resources over an extremely wide area of compensatory education produces only minuscule results. However, as a teacher and department head interested in the development of all children I feel parallel programs such as the Motivation Program must be developed and funded to serve groups of students for their needs.

It has been a pleasure working with the Program.

Cordially,

ISADORE R. KLINGSBERG

APPENDIX   185

                                                           January 15, 1972

Dear Mrs. Segal,

   My assessment of the impact of the Motivation Program ("M" 1965 West Phila. High School) on my subsequent education can only be phrased at this point in terms reflective of the broad overview—as opposed to a more detailed recollection—to which my somewhat distant perspective limits me. It has been seven years since graduation reduced my high school experiences to memories and although seven years is a very short period of time, as I stand near the end of my formal education I must say that seven years is a very long period of experience. The word "education" has come to mean many different things to me since that time, and events and ideas, both in and out of formal education, have to a great degree blurred the reasons for the feeling of educational and intellectual sufficiency, obtained as a bonus to my regular high school curriculum, that I can well remember having during the first few years after leaving the Program. But there are a few memorable aspects of the first "M" Program which I can say with certainty did make tangible contributions to my postgraduate education.

   The first thing that comes to my mind are the special English courses which emphasized speed reading and reading comprehension. Having done my undergraduate work at Temple University where the competition was keen to begin with, and having selected a curriculum which was probably the most strenuous one could take, I know that I might not have been able to stay atop the voluminous required reading much less make the Dean's List several semesters, had I not been introduced to the required reading techniques in high school. This is especially true in light of the fact that I was competing against students whose backgrounds were substantially unlike mine. For example I can remember always having been a relatively slow reader until about 1964 or '65. But from grammar school until college I could be assured that no matter how slow a reader I was, the overwhelming majority of my classmates were slower. Until college my position had always been one of never having to dig deep for the full extent of my potentiality because the partial effort would always suffice to make me one of the top students in my classes. Stifled is he who can exceed others without ever having taxed himself to the limits of his own ability because he will never know how much he can achieve. It wasn't until college and of course law school that I learned what it was like, in the vernacular, to "bust one's hump," for a "C." My college classmates for the most part came from environments that were much more culturally advantageous than mine. So while I was made to spend a summer reading the epics of English literature I was doing something that my college classmates did during the regular school semester as part of their English studies. Hence while attempting to digest several paperback political treatises one day before an exam, or forging through a novel at 1 A.M. in the morning, or perusing *The New York Times* right before a class discussion on world events, etc., I could appreciate the opportunity I had in high school to attend special classes designed specifically to teach specially selected students how to build their reading skills. (The irony now I suppose is that one of the first things you learn in law school is to unlearn your speed reading habits because the law can only be digested very slowly.)

Another memorable aspect of the Program was the cooperation between parents, teachers and administrators who, even in the Program's first years, developed a working relationship unmatched by the traditional PTA-type efforts. My present assessment of this relationship would be that it dispelled the notion that only the affluent care about the education of their young. Today when people like myself spend many hours trying to discover what keeps today's parents so occupied that they do not have the time or concern for the educational, emotional and social needs of their own children it is good to think back to the "M" Program which somehow provided (and I suppose still provides) that needed stimulus, whatever it is. Perhaps this idea of "total family–total educational hierarchy" cooperation and involvement in specialized training is an approach which could provide the answer for which our local community is groping.

Today the Program is probably very different from the one I knew, with new techniques, approaches and activities. I suppose my recollections of the Program in its infancy are now dwarfed by the present city-wide effort and the expansion of programs such as my special reading courses into other fields such as science and math. I suppose "M" '65's occasional junkets to area colleges and universities have been long since replaced by actual student participation in outside occupational and educational fields of student interest. But one of the aspects of the Program that affected me most was the fact that from a very early date in my high school education I was considered to be of college potential and nurtured accordingly. This created a sense of pride since I always knew that someday I would be a lawyer and that first I would have to tackle four years of college. It also prevented the inferiority complex I inevitably would have developed by not having attended one of the city's better high schools. I say this because today it is quite fallacious to tag all high school achievers with the words "college material." College is only for those who, at the high school age, feel they have something to gain from it. It is not a choice to be dictated by parents and teachers, as well-meaning as they may be. Good high school students will not necessarily "grow" into the mood for college within four years after high school graduation. A person may not be emotionally desirous and educationally prepared for college until many years after high school. Yet in high school he may be just as motivated as the college hopeful. It is only when the individual is ready that he should attend. I've met literally hundreds of students in college who had absolutely no business being there. "Motivation" does not mean today what it meant to me in 1965. I can only hope that today's Program seeks to motivate all conscientious students (and their parents) who seek to make the most out of their high school years in terms of bettering themselves and their communities, and who want the professional aid that the Program can offer in finding the post high school option—be it in the realm of an occupation, training or advanced studies—that fits them best.

                Sincerely,

                FRANK FINCH
                "M" '65

THE SCHOOL DISTRICT OF PHILADELPHIA
BOARD OF EDUCATION
PARKWAY AT TWENTY-FIRST STREET
PHILADELPHIA, PENNSYLVANIA 19108

March 6, 1972

Mrs. Rebecca Segal
Specialist for Motivational Programs
The School District of Philadelphia

Dear Rebecca:

The aspects of the Motivation Program which gave so many West Philadelphia High School students a chance at success, happened, I am convinced, because the projects were directly connected with students' needs, interests, and aspirations.

As the vice-principal in charge of the higher education awards, I saw, first hand, the dramatic increase in that first "M" class of pupils going to college. Many of them have already completed a full education. I believe this program deals with the emotional and psychological development of the child on the secondary level and that the exposure to what is good and wholesome in our culture is needed.

From my early observations, the Motivation parents became as active as they did because they were concerned with cultural, leisure and communicating activities neglected in our curriculum.

Since my life has been spent in music and the arts, I consider this area of prime importance. The present secondary education program has neglected humanitarian and cultural aspects of an individual's life. I believe all students on all school levels should be motivated in this way and decry the lack of cultural experiences for the non-college-bound student, such as are provided for the Motivation students.

Sincerely,

ALEC WASHCO, JR.
Member, Board of Education

3 March 1972

Mrs. Rebecca Segal
Motivation Specialist
Philadelphia Board of Public Education

My Dear Rebecca:

The value of the Motivation Program has manifested itself in many ways to us as parents of a Motivation student and as citizens interested in the education of our youth.

As parents, we witnessed in our son an awareness of the Arts that we could not have given him. In other students, we saw evidence of pride, hope and accomplishment that happened only because of their involvement in the Motivation Program.

With kindest personal regards, we are,

>Most sincerely yours,
>
>CHARLES BORKON
>LILLIAN BORKON

THE PHILADELPHIA TRIBUNE
THE CONSTRUCTIVE NEWSPAPER
520 SOUTH SIXTEENTH STREET
PHILADELPHIA, PENNSYLVANIA 19146

March 6, 1972

Mrs. Rebecca Segal
Motivation Specialist
Philadelphia Board of Education

Dear Mrs. Segal,

As you know, I have had several occasions in recent years to observe the Motivation Program at close range while working on feature article for the *Tribune*. At your request I am writing to let you know some of my observations of the program.

I have invariably found the Motivation students to be (if you'll pardon the expression) well-motivated, enthused and intimately involved in the process of education, certainly far more so than non-Motivation students. As a product of the Philadelphia public school system myself as well as a lifelong resident of Philadelphia, I am thoroughly familiar with the lamentable state of public education in this city although by no means do I feel all the blame should devolve on the school administrators (corrupt, greedy and racist politicians are due for a lion's share, I feel).

In spite of these obstacles, though, I believe the Motivation Program has performed wonders with students who were often thought to be uneducable but who were in fact average (and in some cases above average) kids whose talents and potential ability had never been properly harnessed. I have seen the Motivation Program harness this potential in too many cases to make it seem mere accident, chance or coincidence. I have seen enthusiastic teachers and students challenging each other in a learning experience that is heartening at least and charged with electricity and love at best.

I will never forget the Motivation students at Bartram who told me they were on the verge of dropping out of school with flunking grades but who entered the Motivation Program and later earned all A's and B's with expressions of joyous optimism about their future at college. I can only hope that the powers-that-be will see the wisdom of expanding the Motivation Program as widely as is humanly possible and will eventually include in it the thousands of Philadelphia high school students who so desperately need it.

      Sincerely,

      LEONARD LEAR
      Staff Reporter-Photographer

FRANKFORD HIGH SCHOOL
OXFORD AVENUE AND WAKELING STREET
PHILADELPHIA, PA. 19124

March 8, 1972

Mrs. Rebecca Segal
Instructional Services
School District of Philadelphia

Dear Rebecca:

Let me tell you what I like about the Motivation Program.

First and foremost the hopeless kids are my bag. Then I find that when they are singled out in a positive way, as they are at Frankford High, given the extra attention in the small class in an intimate setting, there is benefit to the kids and the school. We have girls with good potential, for instance, who would have dropped out. As it is, the personal attention of the coordinator and the teachers convinced the students to take commercial academic and they are performing well.

Finally, I like the fact that the "M" program benefits the whole school by moving within it and sharing some of its benefits.

>   Marvin Schuman
>   "M" Mathematics Teacher
>   Roster Chairman

March 2, 1972

Dear Mrs. Segal

The fact that I'm probably one of the most sophisticated seniors on Penn State's Campus where the Arts are concerned is due totally to the "M" Program at West Philly High. The cultural section of the program "urged" but it also ruled that every one of us had to attend two kinds of cultural activities each month. This "gentle pressure" was evidently what I needed because I attended operas, ballets, plays and lectures among many other events. What we read or learned in class, often very drily, took on a life of its own on the stage or in a Host Visit with a professor of Chinese history, for instance.

The "M" office was "our place"; we went there to meet and talk to faculty. That's when we saw some of them as real people! We could meet with the other kids to plan for events, shows, politics, school needs and talk just about life in general.

The longer I live away from those high school days, the more I see that what I got from the "M" Program was a willingness to experience everything, try everything, people, art, books.

On a more personal note—I've made my decision about my future and I'd like to discuss my plans with you. I've decided on the rabbinate and I plan to take my first year at Hebrew University in Jerusalem.

>   Sincerely,
>
>   William N. Borkon
>   "M" '68
>   Penn State 1972